NO TURNING BACK

___?___ floor

— plague → mat   — Kiva → "church"
                              sacred worshipping
                              places

— ~~[scribbled out]~~

— Spider Clan & Bear Clan

— **potsherds**

— enforce "white man" ways

Polingaysi shaping pottery at Flagstaff in 1957

No
Turning
Back

A TRUE ACCOUNT OF A HOPI INDIAN GIRL'S STRUGGLE
TO BRIDGE THE GAP BETWEEN THE WORLD OF HER PEOPLE
AND THE WORLD OF THE WHITE MAN

by Polingaysi Qoyawayma

(Elizabeth Q. White)

as told to Vada F. Carlson

THE UNIVERSITY OF NEW MEXICO PRESS
ALBUQUERQUE

© 1964 by the University of New Mexico Press
All rights reserved
Manufactured in the United States of America
Library of Congress Catalog Card Number 64-7652
International Standard Book Number 0-8263-0439-7
Seventh paperbound printing, 1991

FOREWORD

Visiting writers, anthropologists, archeologists, and other friends have insisted for years that it was my duty as an articulate Hopi to tell the world something of my cultural background and my long struggle to span the great and terrifying chasm between my Hopi world and the world of the white man.

Not until the publication a few years ago of a book that defamed the character of the Hopis as a nation, however, was I jolted out of my complacency and into full realization of my responsibility.

Hopi people are exceedingly sensitive to ridicule, and I am no exception to this rule. It has been a ball and chain, preventing me from expressing myself, especially along the line of my painful experiences as a pioneer in Indian education, both as a student and as a teacher.

Now I realize that white people cannot know the truth of the situation unless someone makes it known to them. I also know that a great deal of misinformation that one sees in print is as much the fault of the Hopi informant as of the white writer. In my own experience I have had three different answers to the same question from three different Hopis. This is not to say that each was not convinced that he was telling the truth. It was merely that they were of different ages and from different villages, where rituals varied.

I accept the reasoning of my white friends. They say that I am a good example of what takes place when a person is uprooted and forced to adjust to a new way of life, because I was an ordinary Hopi child at the time education was brought to us through the white man's schools, and because I had only limited experience with white people. (As a family we had known the white Voth family, who came to our village of Oraibi in 1893, when according to my officially determined birthdate I was only one year old.)

Also, they point out, my experience was typical of Indian children of my era and, to a less drastic degree, of Indian children of today. They also argue that because I continued in the educational field, facing problems of bringing Indian beginners into conventional school procedures, I should be more than ordinarily capable of understanding their problems.

It has been painful to recall my long-drawn-out struggle in living. Many of the episodes, buried deeply, emerged slowly. However, now that the effort has been made, I am grateful to my good friends who insisted that this account be written. I am especially grateful to Miss Marion Bowen, and to my biographer, Mrs. Vada F. Carlson, who has had the patience and skill to weld my reminiscences into manuscript form.

My grandmother, prophetic woman that she was, used to say: "It is to members of Coyote Clan that *Bahana* [white man] will come, within your day, Polingaysi, or within the day of your seed, and you of Coyote Clan will be a bond between the *Bahana* and the Hopi people." I am Indian enough at heart to believe that her prophecy has been fulfilled.

POLINGAYSI QOYAWAYMA

NO TURNING BACK

ONE

THE SMALL, brown-skinned woman in the red dress stopped her car in the desert valley and, getting out into the hot sunshine of early autumn, lifted black eyes to the ruins of the ancient village of old Oraibi, once many-storied and proud, a stronghold of the Hopi Indian nation.

Her face, broad and strong-featured and remarkably unlined in spite of the fullness of her years, gave no hint of the emotion welling up in her. Only a sudden glint of tears and the lifting of one hand to her constricted throat told her heartache, her indecision and confusion.

"That is my home."

She murmured the words lovingly, her gaze noting the uneven line the falling stone houses made against the blue sky. "Yes," she thought, "in that place of ruins is the evidence of my beginning. My roots are there. A part of me is there still, in the old home of my parents, in the hill house of my grandmother, in the very dust that whispers in the streets where I played so long ago. Is that where I belong, now?"

As though stirred into action by the intensity of her thought, a whirlwind formed lazily in the sand dunes bordering the valley road. Carrying its load of dust, it spun upward and came swirling and dipping toward her.

1

She held out her hands to it.

"Yes? Tell me, tell me," she said.

But the eddy disintegrated, the dust returned to the desert floor. A fringe of the whirlwind lifted her black bangs, square-cut in Hopi fashion across her forehead. Her skirt fluttered around her legs. But if a spirit of her ancestors moved in the whirlwind, as Hopis believe they do, it had no answer for her.

With a sigh she got back into the car and drove on toward the new village that had grown like a shoot from the ruins above it.

When she was a child the village on the mesa had teemed with activity. During days like this she and the other little ones would have been roaming the talus slopes below the sandstone cliffs, looking for potsherds or hunting rabbits. Now the children of the old village were down here, attending school with those who lived in the newer settlement.

They were in the schoolyard when she passed—black-haired, brown-skinned, bright-eyed. She drove on through the village and headed the car uphill.

An excitement grew in her as she reached the mesa and turned off the highway into the dirt road that led to the ancient village. She was at once eager and reluctant to revisit her childhood home. When she stopped in the gray clay street which was bordered by gray stone buildings that were still occupied despite their age, she made no move to leave the car, but sat waiting.

On one of the nearby housetops an old man, aroused from his nap by the sound of her car's motor, sat up, looked down, then rose stiffly and came down the stone steps and across the plaza toward her. He had a look of great age. His dark skin was weathered and wrinkled. His shabby clothing hung loosely about his small, bony frame. A folded red scarf bound his graying hair. His eyes brightened with interest as he drew near. This, his glance seemed to say, was no white tourist, intent on taking pictures of

2

him, and shouting at him as though he were deaf. This was one of his own people.

The woman in the car smiled at him almost shyly.

"I am happy to find you well, Chief Tawaquaptewa," she said, speaking to him in the Hopi language and with the deference due the hereditary chieftain of the village. "I am Polingaysi, of this village. Perhaps you have forgotten me. I have been away for a long time."

"Polingaysi! Oh-ee-e! You are the little one who wanted to be a white man."

The words were spoken matter-of-factly and without censure, but they brought tightness to the woman's throat and sadness to her mind.

For a moment she could not speak.

"I have come back to visit my old home," she said then, "with your permission."

"You are welcome. Stay as long as you like," the old chief said graciously. "I think you will find things much changed. It is a long time since you were a child here, and sad things have happened."

"I know."

For a moment their eyes met in understanding and mutual commiseration, then the old man stepped aside and Polingaysi got out of her car.

She walked back into the ruined section of the village, her heart crying out: "Yes, much has happened since I was a child. But I am still a child. A lost child. I cannot find my way. Where is the pathway of peace? Where can I find the harmony of the true Hopi?"

She walked unerringly to the jumble of rocks that once had been her home on the mesa's western edge. One small room—and there had been so many of them crowded into it. The roof had leaked like a sifter basket during every rainstorm. This space beside the house had been the storage room. Often it had been empty, or nearly so.

She had spent much of her time at her grandmother's tall house up the street. She walked toward it up the slight grade, noting the walls of ruins that projected below the ruins that had been in use during her childhood.

When the first stone houses were built on this mesa there had been no hill here, no mound of tumbled rocks and sand between the west side of the mesa and the eastern side where the villagers, large and small, in the time of her childhood said their morning prayers to Father Sun and Great Being.

There had been four stories in her grandmother's house. First the dark room of the rain priests, now filled with rubble and who knew what wonderful pieces of old pottery, then what had been called the ground-floor room in her youth, then the second room for general use, and the topmost one for storage and summer sleeping. Four stories, though few people knew about the room of the rain priests, and so thought of the place as three-storied.

Polingaysi climbed the narrow stone steps that led to the one remaining rooftop. The upper story had been razed for building material, or had fallen.

Many times in her childhood she had stood on this very spot, in the corner near the earthen chimney pot whose bulging sides were blackened by smoke from cooking fires of days long past. At first in baby nakedness, later in her first little "birdie" dress of black wool woven by her father, later, after initiation into the mysteries of the Kachina cult, in her one-piece blanket dress.

In the vanished upper room, the grinding stones, the *matas,* had been placed side by side—the coarse-grained ones, the fine-grained ones. Head cocked, small body stiffly still, Polingaysi listened. Could she hear a voice singing the corn-grinding song, or was it only an echo from her remembering heart?

4

Oh, for a heart as pure as pollen on corn blossoms,
And for a life as sweet as honey gathered from the flowers,
And beautiful as butterflies in sunshine.
May I do good, as Corn has done good for my people
Through all the days that were.
Until my task is done and evening falls,
Oh, Mighty Spirit, hear my grinding song.

The old woman who had cared for her so tenderly during her childhood lived again in Polingaysi's thoughts.

Slowly, in her fancy, the tiny, short-legged, brown-bodied desert child she had been emerged and ran down the village street, matted black hair blowing. And it was a hot day in midsummer.

The child joined other children who played in the shade of the rock houses. She dug in the sand with them, cuddled her own family of sheep's-bone dolls, played the game of comparing designs on potsherd dishes. But only fleetingly. Always restless, the little Polingaysi jumped to her feet, brushing dirt from her bare bottom as she said, "I'm hungry. Let's play 'begging-for-food.' "

The others goodnaturedly abandoned their playthings to follow her. Polingaysi chose a home where she knew melons had been stored. With confidence the group began dancing as they sang the begging song.

Please give us some of your melons,
We are hungry and would like to eat something.
Please give us some of your melons to eat.

The Hopi mother came out with a basketful of small melons, gathered for that very purpose, and placed a cool, colorful melon in each pair of outstretched hands. Giggling delightedly, the little ones ran to the edge of the mesa with their gifts. Sitting down on flat rocks, they breathed on their melons, saying "Ah-n-noo-oo!" as a wish, or prayer, that the melons they held would be sweet and ripe. Again the Hopi way of giving thanks for a bountiful harvest had been observed, in this sharing of food with the village children.

Then, in Polingaysi's drifting thoughts, it was evening of that hot day. When darkness brought no relief from the heat, those same children danced for rain.

She, the leader, had only to say, "Come. Let's be cooled," to obtain a following.

"Oh-ee, oh-ee," they cried, trotting obediently after her. "Let us dance for rain."

Water was scarce on the mesa. Each day the women went to the spring below and carried back the meager supplies in *wigoros,* water jugs, of clay. But Polingaysi's grandmother loved her. She would share her precious water unselfishly. Yes, to the last drop. It was to her house Polingaysi hurried.

> Come here, little rain drops,
> Pour on us, pour on us.
> *Anoshka-eh. Anoshka-eh.*
> Pour on us water. Pour on us water.

So the children sang, stamping, turning, until the old song was finished. Then they lined up with their bare backs toward the door, hugging themselves as they bent over to receive the deliciously breathtaking shock of the cool water the grandmother would dribble over them.

Standing alone on the rooftop, it seemed to Polingaysi that she could feel the presence of the Old Ones, and a chill raced over her in spite of the heat. Her mother and her grandmother had been quick to sense and acknowledge the presence of departed ones.

A lifting of mist from the valley, the flowing of a gentle breeze across the mesa, had been enough to alert them. At those times they were wont to say fondly, "Oh-ee. Yes, they are here. They are visiting their homeland."

Many times in her childhood Polingaysi had stared down into the valley, seeking to make out the figures of the visitors. The wind was forever moving the sand of the dunes down there, uncovering ancient cooking pots and hand stones and arrowpoints. Her people had lived there, near the creek which had become a deeply incised wash. All over the valley they had left their record of occupancy, and on the mesa across the wash there were extensive ruins left by those who had vanished centuries before.

Hopi people clung to the past as they clung to the old word *anoshka-eh,* whose meaning had been lost, but which still carried in its utterance some essence of goodness.

In this time, as in her youth, Hopi people believed in strange sights and sounds. Some of them even claimed to have seen Masau-u, God of Death, making his rounds of the village. Wild, destructive Masau-u! Like death itself, he could visit the village at any time he chose, even during the month of December, known to the Hopis as Ka-muyua, the Quiet Moon, or, as some say, the Moon of Dripping Blood, when the entire earth is sacred.

Polingaysi's parents had taught her to observe this period of sacredness with respect, lest evil befall her. There must be no digging into the earth, no stamping upon it, no beating of drums, no loud talking. Muyingwa, the Germinating God, busy under the earth's crust, must not be disturbed in his work of germinating seeds for next season's crops.

Maidens in the grinding rooms must not speak to those who appeared at the watching holes in the walls, sweethearts must go uncourted by the young men, and no one must cut hair. Evil spirits were thought to be waiting to snatch clippings in which to make their nests. Should it be necessary to walk in the dark streets, protection should be sought by making crosses on forehead and the soles of the feet with ashes. If it was suspected that ghosts were entering the houses, pitch was burned to make a sooty veil through which the intruders could not find their way.

During this month, the men spent much of their time down in the warm kivas, praying for long life as they made feathered prayer sticks for future "planting" at the village shrine. This was a way of saying that all life is a planting, a growing, and a harvesting; that prayers are tangible things when properly conceived, and capable of coming to abundant fruition and seedtime.

Seeds for the next spring's planting were collected at the village doorways and carried to the kiva to be ritually blessed and reverently presented to Father Sun by the priests before being returned to their owners. And all during that night One-Horn and Two-Horn priests stood guard over the kiva, for nothing must disturb this fertility rite.

Polingaysi well remembered the ghostly winter nights, the storytelling at the fireplace, the yearning for warm days and the relaxation of tension.

There were good times and bad on the mesa, and at one time there was no food in their storage room. There had been a drought and no crops had been harvested. Water jars were often empty and the village springs were almost dry. People clawed through refuse piles looking for kernels of corn they had discarded in more prosperous times. Hungry children cried themselves to sleep at night.

Polingaysi remembered how sad her strong-bodied mother had been, and how she had gone despairing to the mesa's edge one night to gaze at the flat-topped butte called Soul's Resting Place, as though desiring relief in death from her hardships. Gravefaced but resigned, she had returned.

"I will take a drink of water to weigh me down," she had sighed, then she had stretched out on her sheep pelts to spend the night beside her hungry brood.

The violent, driving rainstorms of summer had always made the brush-and-mud roof leak. At such times the family crouched together under whatever shelter the room provided.

One evening, while water still dripped from roof to plastered floor, Polingaysi had snatched up a blanket and clutching it about her thin shoulders had run outside to the baking pit. This primitive oven of flat rocks was near the house. In it Sevenka, Polingaysi's mother, had baked corn cakes for the family and some of the ashes were still warm and dry. Into them Polingaysi wriggled her feet, and leaning against the warm rocks of the pit she looked up wonderingly into the night sky where stars were beginning to shine.

It was then that a glimmer of hope came to her with the thought that she could better her condition, and that of her family, when she grew a little larger. It was, perhaps, the first stirring of ambition.

Once more the woman looked down at the great expanse of the valley and at the jutting blue buttes that edged it, then she went back down the steps of her grandmother's house and around to the plaza.

This was the *kisonvi,* center of many houses, where the people of Oraibi had for centuries carried out their ceremonial rituals. In the winter, there had been the coming of dear old Uncle Soyal for the children to look forward to. And there had been the colorful Batsavu. How beautiful had been the great baskets of pale green bean sprouts, symbolizing an overflowing harvest! How impressive the procession that came from the north into the village, the watchful guards prancing with whips in their hands and turtle shells clanking on their legs.

Thought of that ceremonial brought up a long chain of related memories. Of mudhead clowns awakening the children with their morning cry and entertaining them with lighthearted antics. Of the Kachinas delivering sheafs of bean sprouts to be cooked and eaten in anticipation of the harvest to come. Of baking dishes full of steaming *pikami,* the sweet corn pudding which was always served on ceremonial occasions.

The equally beautiful Niman Dance, the Going Home Dance of the Kachinas, usually performed in late July, had also never failed to fascinate her.

Not so the Snake Dance, performed in what was called the *dip-keah,* or womb, plaza at the west side of the village. The rite of entertaining the brothers of the underworld had always seemed to her at once profoundly moving and terrifying. Even now, thinking of dancing men with writhing snakes held between their lips made her uneasy. She darted quick, fearful glances to right and left, as though she feared that some beady-eyed snake child, neglected by the gatherers, stared at her with reproachful, vengeful eyes.

Suddenly, Polingaysi realized why the *kisonvi* seemed so deserted and desolate. A sacred shrine, the *bahoki,* had always held a prominent place here. Now it was gone. It had been the heart of the village—on that *bahoki* the prayers of the people had been placed. Who had dared remove it? The essence of the past must still be clinging to those stones, wherever they were.

No wonder the village was lifeless and mouldering—its heart had been stolen. How could it be expected to survive without a heart? Lines of sadness etched Polingaysi's face.

"The blame is partly mine," she confessed to herself. "I am Hopi. Because I am Hopi, I have responsibilities. By breaking the cultural pattern in my own life I have, at least indirectly, helped to destroy it for the Hopi people as a whole. I know not where the *bahoki* has been taken, but I accept my responsibility for its disappearance. Would I be better off had I never broken away from my heritage? Would I do differently if it were possible for me to live my life over?"

Again, she found no answer to her questions.

The love of beauty and the desire for food had motivated much of her early life. Her stomach was forever demanding food. She had been especially hungry one year when the Niman Kachinas came to perform the old ritual of leave-taking. Crouched between her mother and her older sister, she had watched the masked men stride into the *kisonvi,* their arms filled with stalks of sweet corn fresh from the gardens, early melons, and rolls of red *piki.* As they placed the gifts on the ground in the center of the *kisonvi,* Polingaysi savored it mentally. The new corn would be delicious. Oh, but the melon! How sweet the juice of it would be! And the *piki* would be good, too. It was difficult to decide which she most preferred.

While the Kachinas danced, and while the Kachinmanas, the ones dressed as women, made rasping music with their squash shells and notched sticks and deer shoulder blades, she anticipated the gift of food. But when the dancing ceased and the distribution of the gifts began, sudden fears beset her. Suppose they had no gift for her. Suppose she had to return home empty-handed.

She edged forward a little, hopefully. A small Kachina, about the size of her father, looked her way. He came to her. He held out a melon. She took it in her thin arms and hugged it to her, feeling its coolness, thinking of its sweetness, and loving the Kachinas with all her heart.

For fear her mother would scold her, she said nothing about her feeling for the supposedly supernatural beings who would go home to their legendary retreat on the San Francisco Peaks at the end of that day, so she had been told, to stay until the beginning of a new year. She reasoned that since her father was of Kachina Clan, making her a child of the Kachinas, she would be welcomed at that home of the Kachinas where there would always be quantities of food. Besides there was the Mother Kachina to take care of her.

She told no one of her plan to follow the visitors home that evening, but when the dance ended at sunset she sped away from the plaza. She raced along the street to her own house and climbed breathlessly to the roof. The Kachinas disappeared, single file, over the mesa's edge and Polingaysi waited for them to reappear in the valley, which would be her signal to follow at a discreet distance.

Her mother and sister came home. Evening shadows lengthened. Still the valley was empty. Reluctantly, she gave up the vigil.

Not yet initiated into the Kachina cult, she had no idea that the dancers had removed their masks and costumes, discharmed themselves, and entered the village from another direction. She took it for granted they had made themselves invisible to human eyes, and she was happy that they had walked among her people for a little while, in flesh-and-blood reality.

The rhythm of the dance and the throaty chanting of the Kachinas filled her mind. They had danced for rain. She looked up; there was not a cloud in the sky. She puzzled about that, briefly, as she went back down the stone steps.

TWO

DURING HER EARLY childhood, Polingaysi had enjoyed the feeling of security that was the heritage of the Hopis. Her navel cord had been tied to a stirring stick and firmly thrust into the wattled ceiling to serve forever as the marker of her birthplace. While she was still an infant, her ears had been pierced as evidence that she was a Hopi. She had been accepted by her grandparents, named Polingaysi, Butterfly Sitting Among the Flowers in the Breeze, and presented to Father Sun on the twentieth day of her life, then honored by the community.

She was a member of her mother's Coyote Clan, and a child of her father's Kachina Clan. She belonged. She was a Hopi.

Like other children of the old village, Polingaysi spent her little girlhood playing. She dug holes in the moist sand, built tiny rock houses, hunted for broken bits of pottery to use for play dishes. Each spring she went with the mothers and children to gather greens. Gradually her back grew strong enough to carry a little *wigoro* up from the deep funnel of the spring where the water serpent lived. Eventually she began helping to care for the smaller children in her family.

The white man came, but she did not remember the first one she had ever seen. She was shy, but she was not afraid of them, for her father did not fear them. He worked for the Mennonite missionary, H. R. Voth, and whenever possible Polingaysi tagged along after her father, often carrying with her one or more of her flat Kachina dolls made of cottonwood root and adorned with bright paint and feathers.

She enjoyed attending religious services, for she loved to sing, and the missionaries were teaching the Hopi children many songs. Knowing not a word of English, they mouthed the strange syllables.

"Deso lasmi, desi no," Polingaysi sang. The words were, "Jesus loves me, this I know," but she had never heard of the Great Teacher.

Hopi equivalents of the strange syllables added up to, "The San Juan people are bringing burros," and this sent the children into gales of giggles. They agreed the white man was very silly to sing about San Juan people bringing burros, but the *Bahanas* gave them candy after the singing lessons, and the candy tasted good. Besides, whatever the words, Polingaysi loved to sing and to be where things were happening.

One morning she was to have her breakfast of corn cakes, *piki* bread, and water in her grandmother's house before going to the missionaries' services. She knew it was the duty of the youngest member of a Hopi family to feed the family gods and she was the youngest present, but she was in a hurry to be off and would have neglected the duty had not her grandmother reminded her.

The family gods, a crudely carved large stone that was supposed to represent a mountain lion, and two smaller carved stones that represented her cubs, were in a dark room above the mysterious kiva of the rainmakers. The kiva was no longer used, but the older children told of strange noises down there, as though ghosts of the old rain priests haunted it.

Never had Polingaysi been able to perform her simple duty without feeling goose pimples rising on her skin, but the thought of the singing, the kind missionaries, and the possible treats helped her to pick up a pinch of sacred corn meal for Father Sun and a pinch of *piki* flakes for the lion and her cubs, and to sidle into the dark room.

"Please don't hurt me," she whispered to the lion, hastily dropping the *piki* flakes before it. "Father Sun and Good Spirit, protect me," she added, tossing the corn meal into the air before backing out of the room and hurrying back to the family.

They sat on the floor. The food was before them, the *piki* on a plaque, corn cakes in an earthen pot, and there was water into which they could dip the *piki*. They bowed their heads, remembering to be grateful for food made possible by the rain that had fallen and the sunshine that had warmed the Hopi fields.

Polingaysi bowed her head, then ate. A few minutes later, she was with the other small children of the village, lustily singing, "Deso lasmi, desi no."

She did not know the missionaries were on the mesa to teach the Hopis the sinfulness of their ways, to lead them from their ancient beliefs into the white man's way of worship. She was too young to have understood, had she known.

From earliest childhood she had been taught to pray. Getting up at dawn and going to the mesa's edge to voice one's thankfulness for life and all good was part of the established Hopi pattern.

Children who stayed in bed were reprimanded. "Would you have Father Sun carry you on his back?" they were scolded. Sometimes cold water was doused on them. Sometimes a maternal uncle would be sent to rouse them from their warm beds.

"Come now! I am your uncle, and have the right to punish you. Get up at once," he would say, and sleepy-eyed and ashamed, they would obey.

Those were the days of the hereditary Bear Clan chieftain, Lololoma. Often he would be sitting on the mesa's edge, wrapped in his blanket, praying with his face turned eastward long before the others came straggling out to join him.

"Why does he always sit there?" Polingaysi asked her mother.

15

Sevenka tried to explain.

"He is responsible for the well-being of our village, and must make a daily pathway for us, his people, through prayer. He calls us his children. We call him our father. He prays for long life, purity, abundant crops, for all of us who live in Oraibi. He prays for rain. He prays for the essence of good in the plants we use, and in the clay we dig and crush for our pottery making, and in the rocks we pile one on top of the other in house building.

"Your father and I are responsible for the well-being of our own home and our children. It is our duty to see to it that our children have a place to live and food to nourish their bodies. It is Lololoma's duty to see to it that we are all fed spiritually. That is why he prays in the mornings, and again in the evenings. He is the father of our spiritual home."

Polingaysi could not remember a time when she had not made her morning prayer, going with mother, cousins, and aunts to the mesa's edge. First, to rid themselves of evils accumulated during the past twenty-four hours, they turned and spat over their shoulders; then cleansed and ready to face the new day, they breathed on the corn meal in their hands their supplications for long life and good health before releasing the meal into the spirit world by tossing it outward, toward the rising sun.

As the first warming rays of the sun slid over the horizon, touching them with golden fingers, they reached out, symbolically drawing the beams to them and pressing them to their bodies, meanwhile inhaling deeply and praying that they might be made beautiful in body, face, and heart. Clothed in the armor of all good and all beauty, and protected from evil, they were strengthened to meet the day and its problems.

It would have shocked Polingaysi, as it shocked her parents and other Hopis, had she been old enough to understand that the missionaries considered them wicked and unsaved. Their religion was not a Sunday affair; it was a daily, hourly, constant communion with the Source, the Creator from whom came all things that were, large or small, animate or inanimate, the power behind Cloud People, Rain People, the Kachinas, and all the other forces recognized and respected by the Hopi people. But at that time the little girl mixed religions as confidently as she mixed Hopi parched corn and the *Bahana's* hard candy.

H. R. Voth, the Mennonite missionary, had built a home for his family on the far side of Oraibi Wash, in the valley below Oraibi, an ancient city said to have been constantly occupied since about 1120. Polingaysi's father, called Freddie by Mr. Voth, because his name, Qoyawayma, was too difficult for English-speaking tongues, made the trip to and from the Voth home daily. He trotted down the steep mesa trail each morning and back each evening, and for his labors made a salary of fifty cents per day.

It seemed not to excite him when other white men, bringing wagonloads of building materials, began the erection of a building on the slope at the foot of the mesa. They were building a schoolhouse, but the word meant nothing to the children of the mesa and their parents. They knew nothing of white man's ways and had never been inside a schoolhouse.

Since nothing had been said to excite her fear, Polingaysi went about her play unalarmed until a morning when her mother, whose voice was customarily low and calm, called out to her in agonized syllables.

"Polingaysi! Come! Come quickly!"

Frightened, Polingaysi gathered up the younger brother she had been pulling on her shoulder blanket and ran home with him. He gurgled with glee at the bouncing ride she gave him and cried when their mother ran to meet them and snatched him from Polingaysi roughly, saying, "Lie down behind that roll of bedding, Polingaysi. I will hide you with a sheep pelt. Hurry."

"Why?" Polingaysi asked in childish bewilderment.

"Do as you're told!" her mother snapped. *"Bahana* is catching children this morning, for the school. Sister is hiding at grandmother's house."

"Catching children!" What a fearful-sounding phrase. It made Polingaysi think of the older boys catching rabbits in snares. Without argument she darted across the room and flattened herself behind the rolled-up sheep pelts and blankets. Her mother covered her and returned to the doorway.

Polingaysi could hear her sick brother whimpering on his pallet beside the fireplace, then she heard a strange voice, speaking a language she did not understand. When the mother made no answer, another man began talking, this time in not very good Hopi.

"He says, tell you we are going to take your children to school. Where are they?"

"That sick boy is all I have, except for the babies," Polingaysi's mother lied. "He is too sick to go away from home."

There was more talk in the foreign language, then the interpreter said, in Hopi: *"Bahana* says the boy doesn't look sick. We'll take him. Come!"

Polingaysi's sick brother wept aloud, but he struggled to his feet and went with the men.

Almost smothered by the time her mother removed the heavy pelt, Polingaysi began at once to beg her mother not to let the men catch her.

"If they take you, they take you," her mother said, her usually gentle voice harsh in her angry helplessness. "What can we do? The *Bahana* does not care how we feel toward our children. They think they know everything and we know nothing. They think only of themselves and what they want. I don't know what they are going to do to our children, down there in that big house. It is not the Hopi way of caring for children, this tearing them from their homes and their mothers."

All that day the village hummed with resentment and fear.

The children who had escaped the school authorities sidled out of their hiding places only to huddle together and run at the first hint of danger.

The *Bahana,* unable to speak Hopi, had brought with him Navajo policemen, carrying guns and clubs, and the Navajos terrified the Hopi children.

The "Foreheads," as the Navajos were called by the Hopi children because they brushed their hair straight back and apparently scorned bangs such as the Hopi wore, were traditional enemies of the Hopi people. Hopi farmers had suffered many a Navajo raid, and had lost their ripe peaches, their new corn and melons, to the raiders. Occasionally a pretty girl was carried off. Small wonder they entertained no affection for the tall, thin-faced Navajos, so different from the peaceful, farming Hopis.

In their play, Hopi children of that day often acted out Navajo raids. Usually this play-acting took place in late summer, after a heavy rain, when all the potholes in the red rock of the mesa were pools of rain water. The potholes made excellent swimming pools.

This was the time of ripening peaches, which the Navajo raiders liked, so the Hopi youngsters would toss a few peaches into a pool, those who were to play the part of Navajos would daub themselves with mud and slick their bangs back from their foreheads, then hide behind the nearest rock or bush, while the "Hopis" got into the pool with the peaches.

At the first sight of a "Forehead" sneaking toward their pool and their peaches, the "Hopis" would set up a shrill warning.

"Foreheads! Foreheads!" they would shriek. "They've come to steal our peaches."

This was the signal. The "Foreheads" would rush the "Hopis," snatching peaches if possible. When a "Forehead" was caught, he had only to duck under water and sweep his bangs back into place to become a "Hopi," whereupon he could change sides in the game.

Because of their long enmity, the Hopi people felt both hurt and insulted that the white man should enlist the aid of Navajos in forcing attendance at the new school.

Polingaysi's father had known what the *Bahanas* were planning, but since he had no answers for the many questions he knew his people would ask, he had kept silent. Actually, he did not know what "school" meant, and he had no inkling of what it would do for his people.

In spite of his pleasant association with the white missionary, Voth, and the red-faced, white-bristled Government man at the school, Polingaysi's small Hopi father was a member of the conservative branch of the Hopi village and as eager as they to retain the ancient culture of his people. It was the so-called progressive group that had consented to adoption of white man's ways.

"When a Hopi becomes a white man," the conservatives said, meaning, of course, when the Indian is willing to take on an overlay of white culture, "he no longer has a face. We want to be Hopis, not white men. We want our children to learn Hopi ways and live by them."

But the white authorities had persuaded Lololoma, chief of the Bear Clan, to sanction their plans for his people. He had, as his people said, "taken the pencil." By making his mark with it, he committed the children of Oraibi to attendance at the new Government school. He had given his promise that they would attend.

The conservatives flatly refused to follow his lead. In the old days there would have been open war, a clash that would have resolved the issue, but times had changed. Warfare would have brought white soldiers. So only stubborn resistance ensued, with anger smoldering in the hearts of both factions—anger which would eventually lead to a wound from which Oraibi would never recover.

The conservatives were angry, and they were afraid. No one took the trouble to talk with them calmly, explaining what was planned for their children and that they were not being jailed. Or, if someone tried, perhaps the language barrier proved insurmountable.

Unfortunate incidents made those first days of recruiting students much worse than they should have been. A maiden was forcibly taken from the home of her husband's mother before her wedding rites had been completed. She had refused to remove her wedding garments for the garment of ticking, called a Mother Hubbard, which was the school uniform, and had wept steadily until Mr. Voth convinced the school authorities she should be exempted.

Polingaysi's older sister had escaped by hiding in her grandmother's house, and she and Polingaysi had orders to run to the grandmother if the police came again.

For the first time Polingaysi turned her thoughts toward the invading school authorities. A quick-moving, intelligent little girl, she could not accept the situation with a shrug, as some of her playmates did. She was stirred. She didn't understand what was going on, but she was intensely interested in it.

Why, she pondered, her smooth brow perplexed, should the children be confined all day to that big house below the mesa? They weren't hurt. They came back up the mesa trail in the evening, talking and laughing, even singing, after being locked up all day. Even her sick brother seemed none the worse for spending a few days there, though he no longer had to attend school, but was back on his pallet, feverish and coughing.

The Navajo police still patrolled the mesa, but she had been clever in hiding. She wondered if perhaps it might be better to allow herself to be caught and have the worry over. It was an irritating thing to have to be on guard every minute, peering around corners before walking down the streets of one's own village, afraid to be oneself, the old self that had been as free and unhampered as the wandering wind.

The conservative faction had devised a scheme whereby the still uncaught children were warned to run for cover at the sound of a certain high-pitched, prolonged call. Polingaysi heard it one day when she was playing on the hill near her grandmother's house. Forgetting her thoughts of capitulation, she fled from the approaching danger.

"Hide me! Hide me!" she screamed, dashing into her grandmother's house only a few steps ahead of her sister and two other village girls who had thus far evaded the authorities. "The *Bahana* comes."

"Sh-h!" her grandmother scolded, taking her by the hand and leading her toward the hiding room. "Are you forgetting how to behave like a Hopi? Be quiet. You are safe here."

The mountain lion and her cubs crouched beside the big *piki* plaque which the grandmother quickly removed from the loose floorstone it covered. Polingaysi shuddered and hung back as the old woman took her arm. She had never before been in the old kiva of the rainmakers. It was black down there, and musty smells smote her flared nostrils. Then she felt the dirt floor beneath her feet and her grandmother released her arm. A spider web brushed her nose, making her want to sneeze.

She heard, rather than saw, the other girls let themselves down into the darkness, but said nothing to them. The grandmother replaced the stone. Gradually her eyes adjusted to the darkness. A tiny ray of light from the air shaft revealed the other girls, huddled in silence. Momentarily Polingaysi expected to hear a scuffle overhead, the sound of gruff voices, and removal of the floorstone. Trembling violently, she imagined how horrible it would be to be pulled screaming out of this blackness and carried off to imprisonment in the school. But no scuffle took place. No sound of voices reached them. Eventually the grandmother removed the stone and helped them out.

The grandmother was angry. Her black eyes were hot with hatred and her thin lips were compressed.

"They dared come into my house," she muttered. "Those Navajos! They pushed me aside when I tried to keep them out. And that fat *Bahana*. The one with white hairs sprouting from his red face. He watched them and said nothing. I think he hoped they would hit me." She breathed hard for a moment, while the girls brushed dirt from their blanket dresses. "They are gone, but they will come back. In time they will catch you."

The very next day Polingaysi's sister and her friends were trapped on the talus slope south of the village and taken to school.

Polingaysi pretended she felt no interest in the striped cotton dress her sister wore home that afternoon, but she was alive with curiosity. It looked clean and pretty. How did it feel? Was it warm, like their blanket dresses?

Pretending unconcern at home, she went to the home of one of her playmates and asked about the new garment.

"Will you let me try it on?"

The other girl was willing. They ran behind the house. Off came Polingaysi's one garment. Off came the ticking dress. On over Polingaysi's black head it went. The other girl was taller. Her dress came to Polingaysi's ankles. She felt grown up in it. She ran her hands over the smooth material approvingly. It was not harsh, like her home-woven wool blanket dress.

"I like it," she said, taking it off and returning it. "Tell me, do the *Bahanas* hurt you, down there in that big house?"

"No," her friend said, with a shake of her head. "They don't do anything to us. We sit on a seat and make marks. We play in the schoolyard. When Father Sun is overhead, they give us food."

"Food? What kind?" Polingaysi asked, for this was one of her favorite subjects. *"Nu-qui-vi? Piki? Som-ev-i-ki?"*

The other girl shook her head.

"*Bahana* food," she said. "I don't know its name."

The next day it seemed to Polingaysi that all the children except herself had gone to school. She was lonely. None of her games held her interest. The simple, ordinary pursuits had lost their tang. Her thoughts were down below, at the school.

"I am not happy," she admitted. "I am lonely."

Casually, she worked her way slowly across the mesa from her own home and sat down on a rock, letting her short legs dangle. She could hear the children calling to each other as they played in the schoolyard. They sounded happy.

She did not have her mother's permission to go down the trail, but down the trail she went, dodging behind rocks and bushes when she met villagers coming up the trail, then sauntering on, nearer and nearer the schoolhouse.

At noon, when the children came out of the schoolhouse again, she was playing beside a nearby boulder. Two of her friends saw her and came running to her. Shy as a little desert animal, she hid from them at first. Though she could no longer endure being left in the backwash of all this excitement, she knew the enormity of her action. No one had forced her to do this thing. She had come down the trail of her own free will. If she went into that schoolhouse, it would be because she desired to do so. Her mother would be very angry with her.

When she yielded to her desire to be with her friends and to savor the new experience at the cost of losing her freedom, the other girls took her hands, and between them, pulling back only slightly, she went to the schoolhouse.

A bell rang. The children lined up and marched past the kitchen where each was given a saucer of syrup, a piece of hardtack, and a tin cup of water. After they had eaten, the bell rang again and they lined up to march into the schoolhouse. The white man with the red face and the white whiskers stood beside the door, hairy hands on his hips. Polingaysi tried to sidle past him, but he stopped her. Her heart pounded like a Hopi drum as he said something to a Hopi girl, several years older.

"He says to take you and clean you up," the older girl said, taking Polingaysi's hand and leading her away. There was a big tub in the room to which Polingaysi was taken. The older girl poured water into it, instructing Polingaysi to undress. She helped her into the tub, soaped her generously, scrubbed her from head to toes, then rinsed and dried her body. As Polingaysi had hoped, the girl then gave her one of the ticking dresses and rolled her blanket dress, tying it with the woven sash.

"Now, go to school," she said when Polingaysi had struggled into the strange garment. "They'll tell you what to do."

The teacher must have been waiting for her. As she hesitated at the door, he came over, took her by the arm, and walked her rapidly to a desk where two other little girls were sitting. He shoved her in beside them and pushed a pencil and a piece of paper in front of her. He was a thin, sour-faced young man with cold, unsympathetic eyes. She could not understand what he said to her before he turned away.

One of the other girls whispered to her, "Make marks like the ones he makes."

The marks the teacher made on the blackboard spelled "cat," but Polingaysi did not know it. She copied them as best she could, filling her paper on both sides.

Climbing the trail with the other children after school, she began to have misgivings. What would her mother say? She had no doubt wondered where Polingaysi had gone and worried about her. On the mesa once more, Polingaysi took a roundabout way home, dragging her bare feet to prolong the painful moment of confession. Her older sister reached home long before she did.

When Polingaysi stepped into the doorway, four pairs of eyes met hers: her sick brother's, sad and reproachful; her older sister's wide with excitement; her mother's sorrowful; and the baby brother's, warm and loving.

Her mother spoke.

"Who took you to school? I looked everywhere for you. The *Bahana* has not been in the village all day long."

Polingaysi hung her head, the rolled blanket dress clutched to her bosom.

"I took myself."

"So! You self-willed, naughty girl! You have taken a step in the wrong direction. A step away from your Hopi people. You have brought grief to us. To me, to your father, and to your grand-parents. Now you must continue to go to school each day. You have brought this thing upon yourself, and there is no turning back."

She turned her gaze away from Polingaysi, emphasizing the finality of her words. A great sadness seized the little girl in the doorway. She had been condemned for committing herself to a new way of life. Tears rushed into her black eyes and spilled over. She dropped her rolled-up bundle and ran to the mesa's edge to shed her repentant tears in solitude.

THREE

Rich in life, color, and emotion, the Hopi way had been a strong but invisible web, holding the people together. Through their ritual dances, through their songs that had been handed down from generation to generation, they were able to express themselves.

In all things, great and small, the true Hopi saw the forces of creation in operation. This spiritual understanding gave a sense of depth and dignity to their frugal and often difficult everyday existence, as did the unfeigned respect of the young people for the wisdom of their elders, and the devotion of the elders in providing the children with mental and spiritual illumination as well as physical sustenance.

The school was a foreign influence, something that stood against the Hopi way of life. *Ka-Hopi.* Not good. How could one cope with these loud-voiced, domineering *Bahanas?*

Accustomed to obeying their parents' low-voiced instructions, the majority of the Hopi children were meek with the white teachers and posed no disciplinary problems. However, some of the boys, keenly aware of the seething resentment of their elders and disturbed by it, became a bit unruly. Retaliation was prompt. A few of them were booted, others were slapped in the face.

Even one such case was enough to arouse the ire of Hopi parents, who do not believe in whipping except ritually by the proper persons and at the prescribed time. During initiation in the kiva, with the child's godfather present to share in the chastisement as evidence of adult responsibility, whipping was permissible, even desirable. But to be chastised publicly, in the school, was a disgrace to child and parents alike.

Polingaysi remembered vividly the punishment of one of her friends. Because the girl did not stop talking at once when told to do so, she was placed on top of the big-bellied stove, unheated at the time, of course, and an eraser was shoved into her mouth. She sat there, stiff with fright, head bent in shame and saliva dripping, until the teacher's sadistic appetite had been satiated.

Polingaysi was too young to understand all that went on that first year in school, but she developed a deep caution, becoming suspicious of the motives of the school personnel and of white people in general, however kindly.

"*Hak-kim-poo-ma-ah!*" the Hopi says, meaning, "I know what they seem to be but I do not know what they are inside."

One day Polingaysi came home with a cardboard hung around her neck on a string. Lettered on it was her new name: Bessie. Her sister Duvangyamsi's new name was Anna. The change of name was merely one more evidence to the girls' mother and grandmothers that the white man was unfeeling.

"You had your beginning as a true Hopi," Polingaysi's mother told her, fingering the cardboard. "You were named in the Hopi way. Your true name is Polingaysi. That will always be your true name."

"I took you, newly born," Polingaysi's paternal grandmother chimed in. "I held your warm body against my bared legs. I presented you with your first Mother Corn. I pierced your little ears. For twenty days I cared for you, observing the traditional manner of caring for a newborn child. Your true home is the house in which you were born. Your navel cord was tied to a stirring stick and thrust into the wattled ceiling of that room where you emerged from the darkness of your mother's womb into the warm dark of your first outer home. That is where your roots are. Your beginning. It was I who named you Polingaysi. It is a beautiful name. It fits you well. Your are a daughter of the Kachinas, as any Hopi will know by your name. This silly name the white man has given you means nothing."

Solemn in the face of this passionate outburst, Polingaysi looked fondly into the grandmother's wrinkled face.

"I am Polingaysi," she declared. "I will always be Polingaysi. But when the *Bahana* calls me Bessie, I will pretend I have forgotten my own name."

Still, it was not easy to make oneself over by government edict. It was much simpler to grow, step by established step, within the pattern of Hopi life.

She still wore her straight black hair loose about her shoulders, the bangs square-cut across her forehead. When she had more years, like Anna, she would receive the *be-lon-so-mi,* or maidenbud, hairdress. Her parental grandmother would wind the loose locks into the tight buds at each side of her head and bind them with a length of hair cord, made from family cuttings.

So she thought, not knowing that she was destined not to wear the traditional hairdress; the maidenbuds would not be for her, nor would she, later on, wear the great whorls of the *poliene,* as would other Hopi girls of marriageable age.

Progress was rolling across the Hopi mesas as relentlessly as the white man's wagon wheels. The Hopis had no defense against it, except ridicule and a spirited scorn. On the schoolgrounds the children were forbidden to speak the Hopi language or to call each other by their Hopi names, but on the way home, to show their contempt for the rules, they delighted in calling out names in the Hopi way.

Confusing the situation even more hopelessly was the fact that the missionaries were doing their best to convince the Hopis of the utter folly and abysmal sinfulness of their ancient beliefs. For centuries, religion had determined the entire structure of Hopi life. To them, life was a constant prayer to the Creator, the Great Spirit. Not just one day a week, but every day, was a day of prayer to the Hopi. They could not be changed overnight.

The old people were frightened. "How can we weave beauty into our ceremonial kilts and sashes if we are hugging hatred to our hearts?" the men asked each other. "Hatred makes you very warm inside, but Good Being doesn't help you when you are warm like that. When you argue with the white man, you just get the worst of it. We are not two-hearts. We must make ourselves endure this thing that is happening. We must give in. We must let the white man learn his mistakes in his own way."

Mothers told their children, "We must not allow the bad behavior of the *Bahana* to cause us to act in the same manner. We must try not to think bad thoughts, because bad thoughts are like jabbing at the thought-of-one with a knife. He can't see what you are doing to him, but you know, and killing someone in your thoughts will let evil spirits into you. We must be peaceful and unresisting. Otherwise, how can we be pure-hearted enough to offer our prayers to Cloud People and the Rain Gods? And if we do not offer prayers and Rain Gods forget us, then surely we shall starve."

The thought of starvation in the village terrified Polingaysi, who had heard many stories of famine though she had not seen the hunger-faces of which the old ones spoke. It was bad enough to have had short periods of hunger, but no food at all? What could be worse?

The most wonderful of all things was food, quantities of food, such as she and her family enjoyed after butchering a sheep. Every edible portion of the animal that could not be dried and stored was cooked and eaten. The liver, heart, kidneys, brains, cleansed intestines and stomach linings—on these the children were allowed to gorge until their stomachs were stretched.

With a new objective, Polingaysi went to the mesa's edge for prayers. In the pink light of new day she searched her heart for bad things she had done, admitted them to herself, then spat them out symbolically, over her shoulder, westward. Then facing the sun with a clean heart, she could feel uplifted. Life was beautiful, and she would be beautiful.

She had watched the old men meditating on the rooftops, wrapped in their blankets. She had seen them cast the blankets aside as the sun rose, had seen them rise and reach out to the sun's rays and press that outpouring of energy to their bodies. Her mother had told her they were praying for health and wisdom, so she too prayed for health and wisdom, bringing the sun's rays to her with passion and bathing herself in them with slow strokings of her brown hands and complete faith in their efficacy. Against the invading white man the Hopis had no other defense. Prayer, prayer alone, was their refuge.

Yet, in their hour of stress, the Hopis forgot their own tenets. They had been warned since infancy against bitter thoughts. They had been told repeatedly that revenge was not for the Hopi, yet friction, smoldering but intense, was developing between Chief Lololoma and Yeokeoma, leader of the Spider Clan.

It was in the Spider Clan kiva that Polingaysi's father first became aware of the dangerous situation. Yeokeoma could not talk of the white man and the Bear Clan's acceptance of him without anger. Lololoma, by "taking the pencil," had betrayed the Hopis, Yeokeoma charged. He would lead them down the wagon road of the *Bahana*. To follow him without protest would be to become slaves. Yeokeoma wanted no compromise with white ways. He wanted to continue in the old way of the Hopi, with no deviation such as schooling. He predicted, and the word spread rapidly, that there would be a time when the issue between himself and Lolo-loma's followers would come to a head.

"When that time comes," he said, "those who wish to follow me will travel the old trails of our people. If we are defeated, we must leave Oraibi. We will go far north to our ancestral village, now in ruins, and live there."

Conceding that Lololoma was a weakling, less resentful men reminded Yeokeoma of the many good things Lololoma was promised by the Great White Father in Washington. For instance, Hopis were to be protected by the military from Navajo and Ute raids, and it was not Lololoma's fault that the Hopis had not yet received the wagons, stoves, and other good things promised in return for his cooperation in the matter of sending the children of the village to school.

It became increasingly apparent as the days rolled by that two such strong ideas could not prevail in one small village. A change was coming, though there was no telling just when it would take place, nor how. "Will we be expected to kill those who oppose us?" one Hopi asked the Spider Clan man. "I have many relatives among Bear Clan."

Yeokeoma stood up, Polingaysi's father later told her, and the expression in his eyes was that of a man who knows his time of trial is not far distant. "Let this be understood," he said. "No blood must be shed."

Outwardly, life went on as usual. But the very elderly Hopis, their own way of life unchanged, noticed the little changes of thought and manner that were taking place among the children and young folk.

One day the villagers had been called to the *kisonvi* by the village crier to hear a long, serious pronouncement by the warrior chief, second in command in the village and a staunch friend of the aging chief. When it was finished, Polingaysi's grandmother began to weep softly, the tears running down her wrinkled cheeks unheeded.

"Grandmother, why do you water the sand with your tears?" Polingaysi asked. "What did Warrior Chief say, that you should be so sad?"

The old lady slowly dried her tears on the edge of her blanket and, after a time of thought, spoke.

"It was not what Warrior Chief said that made me weep. It was what I saw there at the center of many houses. Things are not as they used to be. Warrior Chief spoke in behalf of Lololoma, and perhaps it is true that Lololoma could not prevent the fate that has befallen us. For a long, long time white men have been trying to get a foothold here in Hopiland. The Spanish came. We drove them away. They came again and we drove them away. But there seems to be no way to drive these white men from the mesas.

"It has not been many moons, compared with the length of my life, since these people came, but already I see their influence. The maidens are trying to make their hair look like the hair of the white women, though no hairdress could be more beautiful than the ancient whorls of the *poliene.* The women are laying their blanket dresses aside for the thin cloth dresses the trader sells. At a distance our men look like white men, even to their shoes."

Placing her thin hand on Polingaysi's head she looked into the girl's sympathetic eyes. "I tell you, Polingaysi, you will live to see a time when the *dotsi,* our soft buckskin moccasin, is no longer worn. My own grandmother once told me there would some day be a path made in the heavens and along it people would travel as do the eagles. She said, too, that people would move swiftly, their feet not touching the ground. And she had never seen a man on horseback.

"She said that in that time the Hopis would no longer walk quietly, single file, along their ancient streets, but that they would

33

walk side by side, uttering bad words in loud voices, as the boys and girls are doing today. Girls would conceive before their time of womanhood was proved, and unknown diseases would mystify the Man With Eyes, whose duty it is to heal.

"Minds would be confused. Strangers would dig in our fallen-in ancestral homes and shake the garments of the ancients. We have seen this prediction come to pass.

"When these things happen," the old voice droned on, "it will be the time of *Suh-ah-kits-pe-oo-tani,* the time when changes come swiftly, and that will be the forerunner of the end of an age."

Hypnotized by the portentous words, Polingaysi sat in silence.

"Fortunate is the Hopi who can come home to our village in that day," the old woman said, her voice dropping to a whisper as she visualized the time of which she spoke. "They will come, crawling on their knees up the mesa trail. They will come from the far places to which they have gone. With them will be a white brother and a white sister, the only survivors of their race, and we will give them shelter, though it is foretold that they shall have caused the terror and the death by their magic knowledge.

"This prediction was made by Black Bear Hand many years ago, and Oraibi ruins have now reached the magic number, four, which was said to mark the beginning of the last age."

Standing now on the top of the fourth ruin, as a jet plane trailed white plumes across the blue sky, Polingaysi remembered that day nearly half a century before. The "path in the heavens" had been made. Down in the hot valley where heat waves shimmered, an automobile was kicking up dust. "People will move swiftly, their feet not touching the ground." How true.

Confusion of mind? She knew how horrible that could be. She had suffered it for years because of her break with the old tradition, and she had come back to ask herself one question: "Is this, my ancestral village, where I truly belong?" It was good to feel the stillness of the mesa top, to feel the warm desert air blow through her hair and fan her dark cheek.

As she struggled to merge with the world of the white man, she had missed the sense of direction that had governed her youth. Her Hopi mother had taken nothing for granted. In teaching her daughters, she had included every traditional detail.

For instance, there had been a day when Sevenka had told Polingaysi to make blue cornmeal dumplings for the midday meal. Sevenka supervised as the girl measured handfuls of the blue-gray flour into a pottery bowl and poured hot water over it, stirring vigorously with her own stirring stick.

"Now," she said, as Polingaysi paused, out of breath, "add a little cold water and a portion of this liquid in which I have soaked sage ashes. It will give flavor to the dumplings and a good color. Last of all, add a small pinch of sand."

Polingaysi demurred. "Sand is not good to eat. Why do we always add a pinch of it?"

Calmly, Sevenka explained. "A small portion of food is being prepared for many hungry people. To it we add sand as a prayer for abundance. Sand, whose grains are without number, has in it this essence. What is more plentiful than the sand of Mother Earth in its endlessness? We remember that as we mix our food in its lack of muchness.

"Now, as you knead this dough in your warm hands, bear good thoughts in your heart, that there be no stain of evil in the food. Ask that it may have in it the greatness and power of Mother Earth; then those who eat it will be nourished in spirit as well as in body."

She needed nourishment of spirit now, Polingaysi admitted, her gaze fixed on the slopes of the San Francisco Peaks to the south-west. Nu-va-da-ka-o-vi, her Hopi people called these sacred mountains.

A legend often told by her father's clan concerned the peaks. "Our ancestors, the Kachina People, once lived among the foothills and on the slopes of Nu-va-da-ka-o-vi," it began. "Before they lived there, on the Snowy Heights, they lived near another mountain far to the south where it was warm. When they came north they traveled slowly, stopping to plant corn and raise crops before pressing on. They brought Mother Corn with them from the south. She was small then. The ears were no longer than a man's thumb. That is why, when we come to the time of harvest, the time for bringing the Corn People in from the fields, we gather each tiny nubbin, as well as the dried leaves and the stubble. It is our way of honoring Mother Corn, who has nourished us since times unknown."

Familiarity with this story had made it easy for her to understand a certain long-ago scene. She had been playing at the home of her paternal grandparents when her grandfather came trotting up the street, singing a sacred song and carrying a heavy bundle on his back. Her grandmother immediately ceased grinding meal and went to meet him. He handed her the bundle. She received it tenderly, crooning to it as to a beloved child, and took it at once to the corn room.

Polingaysi followed her and saw her lay the bundle on the floor and open the carrying cloth to expose the tiny ears of corn.

"Thank you, my Corn People," the grandmother said, talking to the nubbins as she laid them in a neat row on the plastered floor. "You have come from far away, but now you are at home. Here you shall remain, and the harvest shall rest on you, for you were in the beginning."

"The Snowy Heights were beautiful in those old days when the Kachina People lived there," the grandmother had once told her. "There was much firewood and there was grass on which the game lived. But, there were also many wolves, bears, and mountain lions. They killed the people. The deep snows taxed the strength of the people and they were sometimes visited by a sickness that took them from life. After a time there were too many gone-away people, so those who remained started out to find a better place to live.

They came to Moencopi Wash and moved eastward, guided by Tso-wi-long, God of Moisture, who lives in the heavens.

"After many moons of traveling they stopped at Shadow Springs, off to the north, old Kisi-wuh. From there, after another great time, they came to Oraibi and were refused four times, though they offered the secret of bringing rain in return for shelter. It was only when drought and famine overtook Oraibi that the proud chief sent for the Kachina People. By that time they had gone back toward Nu-va-da-ka-o-vi.

"You know how Mother Kachina comes now from the east, as she came long ago to be rejected and turned away. You know how she carries a plaque of seeds of many kinds. You have heard her cry out, 'I have traveled a long way and I am weary,' and you have heard the Powamua priest say to her, 'Yes, I know. You must be very tired,' before he takes from her arms the seeds which are a gift from the Kachinas, who brought us food and saved us from starvation in the beginning of time."

The ceremonies of her people were rooted in antiquity. How was one ever to understand their complexity, their hidden meanings? Of one thing Polingaysi, the woman, was certain, the Kachina dances would be the last of the old rites to be discarded. Babies learned the dance steps as they learned to walk. Before their legs were strong enough to bear their weight, they were moved by mother or father in dance tempo. The kiva dancing of the winter months and the plaza ceremonials of summer were so much a part of their life that the chants and rhythm were ingrained, a part of their flesh and blood, as natural as heartbeats. Yet, looking into the future and judging by the swift changes of the past, she felt she could foresee a time when the young people would desert the villages on the jutting mesas and no one would be left to sing the ancient chants and stamp moccasined feet in the ritualistic pattern.

When that time came, the Hopi people would have taken a new pathway. The Kachina masks would no longer adorn the kivas, but would be seen only in museums, and after a time the masks would lose the very essence of the Hopis who had made and worn them.

Progress, white-man style, took strange forms. The red stone church of the Mennonites was one of them. Built by the Reverend Voth in 1901, it stood on the edge of the mesa beyond the flat-topped buildings, a foreign thing with not one feature to blend it with the village. It did not belong there. It was a thing to be ignored, or to be looked at and rejected by the offended eyes of the Hopis.

No doubt it brought to mind that other church of long ago, the San Francisco Mission of the invading Spanish, and the Franciscan priests whose presence stirred the Oraibians to revolt and finally to murder. A mound marked its former location, but its stones had long since been scattered and its heavy beams used in kiva construction, and in the minds of the village people there was a consciousness of those days of hot rebellion against an imposed religion.

There were those among the elders who claimed to know where the murdered priest's remains were buried in the rocks below the mesa, as well as the identity of the men who had killed him and flung him over the cliff.

Even then, it was declared, there had been two factions in

Oraibi, one friendly to outsiders, the other hostile. The quarrel of Yeokeoma and Lololoma was in a sense only a continuation of the village strife.

While they quarreled, life went on as usual. The missionaries continued their efforts to convert the Hopis to Christianity, babies were born, old people died, young people married. The death of Lololoma, which occurred, according to one source, "after the smallpox epidemic of 1901," brought no end to the disturbance between conservatives and progressive factions. Lololoma, knowing that he was "growing small again" in old age, had passed on the rituals and secret knowledge of his station to his nephew, Tawaquaptewa, whom he named as his successor. Tawaquaptewa inherited the quarrel along with the leadership of the village.

Tawaquaptewa had a tall, slender brother whom the white man had named Charles. Charles, a bachelor, decided to take a wife, and though there were many girls who wished to wash hair with him, influential members of Bear Clan looked at Polingaysi's tiny, serious, older sister, Anna, and found her most desirable of them all. She was young by Hopi standards of that day, which required that a bride be well matured and capable of assuming the heavy responsibility of a home and children, but her parents were quietly approached.

There was a scarcity of corn in the Qoyawayma household that winter of 1903-04, and one must have corn if one is to begin grinding in preparation for a true Hopi wedding, but this was not allowed to stand in the way. In a most practical manner the problem was solved by the arrival, at night, of corn-laden burros at the Qoyawayma home.

According to the notations of the Rev. H. R. Voth, Anna and Charles were married in Hopi fashion on March 1, 1904. Charles was much older than his bride and second in line for chieftainship of Oraibi, should Tawaquaptewa die.

Polingaysi's family was now related by marriage to the village Bear Clan leader.

Across the ever-widening Oraibi Wash in the valley, the home of the Voths became a mecca for Yeokeoma and his followers. Not openly, but under cover of darkness, the Spider Clan man and some of his closest followers visited the missionary, seeking to find some gem of wisdom in his teaching that would prove their case.

In their innocence, they confused the word "Messiah" with their own word "Masau-u," Masau-u being the fearful God of Death who has access to Hopi villages at all times and who is capable of destroying opposing forces.

Polingaysi's father saw the tracks of the visitors as he went to the Voth home one morning. He wondered who they were and why they had visited the missionary secretly. In due time he discovered their identities, but he had no idea why they were having midnight talks with Voth until one night when, instead of trotting home at the end of the day, he went to sleep on a bench beside the house. He awakened to hear Yeokeoma talking, and after a moment he joined them. They were curious about his presence, but not offended, continuing their talk undisturbed. After that night, Qoyawayma often talked to Yeokeoma in the kiva.

Essentially, Qoyawayma was a conservative, as was his sturdy wife Sevenka, but he realized the hold the white man had on the mesas and knew in his heart that resistance was useless. He could see the trend the kiva outbursts were taking and was not in favor of bringing the undercover turmoil to its threatened culmination.

Eventually he confided in Sevenka, telling her of his fears and of the brewing trouble. She was disturbed, so much so that she dreamed about the matter.

Dreams play a significant part in Hopi life. Sevenka commanded respect as a member of the Coyote Clan, which is thought to be possessed of extraordinary psychic powers. Her husband respected her dreams and her interpretation of them. Her children were awed by them.

"I will tell you now," she said, on the morning after her dream, "that Yeokeoma and his followers cannot win this struggle. They are already beaten. That I know, because of my dream."

"What was this dream?" her husband asked.

A faraway look came into Sevenka's eyes.

"This village was deserted by Spider Clan and friends of Spider Clan," she intoned. "Their kivas were empty. Their ceremonial possessions were strewn along the streets, torn and scattered as though by violence. There was crying. I asked what had happened and was told that a bear had appeared from the north and had gone into Blue Flute kiva, where our village leaders gather. He was in there splitting the hearts of our people."

Fatalism is a part of Hopi nature. Qoyawayma did not question the truth of Sevenka's dream. What is to be will be, and this was more than a sudden quarrel between two strong leaders. It was a "becoming" of what had been and would be again.

In the beginning, so the old legends relate, the Hopi people came up out of the Underworld because one faction was angered by the behavior of the other. A group of them went on ahead of the main body. Coming to the Little Colorado River, they saw a dead bear, and thereafter called themselves the Bear Clan.

After many wanderings they built homes on the lower slopes of the mesa where the village of Shungopovi now thrives. Being the first Hopis to arrive in this wilderness, Bear Clan leaders laid claim to all the mesas and the lands adjoining them, establishing themselves as leaders and owners.

Two brothers headed Bear Clan at that time—one of them named Matcito. He and his brother began to quarrel over leadership of their village. Matcito left, or was possibly driven out of the village. He established himself in a rock shelter below the mesa top now occupied by the ruins of Old Oraibi. After a time, the story goes, his wife and some of his friends joined him and began the erection of a pueblo on the mesa top, thus founding Old Oraibi.

When Oraibi came into being, all the other Hopi villages were on the slopes of the mesas or in the valleys. Later, for protection, they moved to the tops.

About ten miles distant one from the other, the three Hopi mesas are gigantic outthrusts of rugged, rock-capped terrain extending from the larger mass of Black Mesa. Called by the white man First, Second, and Third Mesas, they are a part of the roughly 4,000-square-mile Hopi Indian Reservation set aside by Executive Order in 1882. This reservation is something like a small island in the large sea of the surrounding Navajo Indian Reservation. High, fortresslike, the little villages stand, whipped by winter winds, burned by summer suns, with Oraibi the most ancient of them all.

First Mesa villages are Walpi, Hano, Sichomovi, and Polacca; Shipaulovi, Mishongnovi, and Shungopovi share Second Mesa; Oraibi, Hotevilla, Bakabi, and New Oraibi are Third Mesa villages, with Moenkopi, forty miles to the northwest, attached to the mother village of Oraibi—the rich sandy land along Moenkopi Wash having been farmed by Oraibi men for many years.

Moenkopi was likened by some Oraibi residents to a sort of colony, since men living in Oraibi regularly planted crops there and walked, or ran, there to cultivate and harvest them.

The bickering that had marked the establishment of Oraibi continued, flaring up, then subsiding, until September 1906, when it became evident that a showdown was unavoidable.

Sevenka, a conservative by nature, might be in danger when the fight erupted, her husband reasoned. Anna, married into Bear Clan, was safe. He, himself, because of his closeness to the missionaries, would not be driven away. To save their home, it seemed best to him to send Sevenka out of the village for the time being.

Until a decision was reached and the turmoil ended, she could take refuge with the Voth family.

Sevenka had the Hopi woman's strong attachment to her home, humble though it was and leaky-roofed. It pained her to pack up her bedding and food and lead her children off the mesa under cover of darkness, but she obeyed her husband. The little flock, each with a bundle on his or her back, left the mesa top near their home, stole quietly around the base of the cliffs and hurried across the valley and the wash to spend the night in the safety of the missionaries' home. Qoyawayma remained on the mesa, an interested spectator during the final hours of Oraibi's greatness.

The Reverend Voth joined him there early the following morning, leaving the women and children at home to worry and wonder. What was happening? Were people being hurt? Killed? Yeokeoma had ordered that no blood should be shed, but in a struggle anything might happen. They looked through binoculars, saw dust rising, but could not make out the figures involved.

Polingaysi, always possessed of a soaring imagination, was terrified by the thought of hearts being literally split by a marauding bear. Her father, she thought with secret horror, might even then be lying in the dust, heartless and bathed in blood. It was after sunset when the men came down the trail together, unharmed, and told those at home the dramatic story of the struggle.

It had begun early in the morning, with Chief Tawaquaptewa taking the initiative. He had ordered the hostile conservative reinforcements from Shungopovi to leave the village, and they, backed by Yeokeoma and his followers, had refused. A rough and tumble scrimmage ensued, with tempers flaring. Yet even in the heat of hand-to-hand combat, the Hopis of both factions remembered their determination to refrain from killing anyone.

By late afternoon of that seventh day of September, the opposing factions were lined up at the northwestern corner of the village facing each other, and Yeokeoma drew with his bare big toe a line running east and west. He grouped his followers behind him to the north, and the progressives, their backs to the village, faced him.

"If your men are strong enough to push us away from the village," he is said to have told Tawaquaptewa, "and to pass me over the line, it will be done. But if we pass you over the line, it will not be done and we shall have to live here."

Yeokeoma thereupon became a human pawn, pushed backward and forward violently until he was finally pushed well over the line to the north. He was severely mauled, and admitted his defeat.

"Well, you pushed me over the line and it is done," he said. "It had to be this way."

Polingaysi's father told of standing beside a man with a loaded rifle. He was a conservative. "Remember Yeokeoma's words," Qoyawayma reminded him. "There must be no spilling of blood." Angered, the man flung the rifle away and joined the fray barehanded.

Blood was shed, however, before the followers of Yeokeoma were bodily pushed out of the village. Women were dragged from their houses, children screamed and cried in terror, and many other terrible things were done, Polingaysi's father said. One man took a baby on a cradleboard and hurled it after its mother. The sturdy cradleboard absorbed the shock as it landed on end and the child was only badly shaken, though its mother was certain it had been killed.

Polingaysi went home with her family, back to the stone house on the edge of the mesa. How still it seemed, that day after the split. Almost every home mourned some dear relative "pushed out" with Yeokeoma. Houses were empty of people, though their belongings remained. They had not been allowed to take them.

Ironically, though their leaders had known this conflict would eventually take place in the legendary pattern, the people were surprised.

It was their good uncle Sinoyva—Running After Flowers—whom the Qoyawayma children missed the most. The little boys, especially Matthew, mourned him. He had been kind and loving, and had allowed them to tag after him wherever he went.

On the day after the fight, September 8, a statement and agreement, composed by the superintendent at Keams Canyon and signed by Tawaquaptewa and his leaders, gave the followers of Yeokeoma the right to come back in groups of not more than three people to remove their belongings to the site, seven miles away, where they had stopped to rest and where they would remain to establish the village of Hotevilla.

It was several days before the ones pushed out began coming back, timidly at first, then more boldly as the feeling against them became less heated. Sinoyva came as soon as he could and stayed as long as he dared, weeping when he was forced to leave the clinging children.

"It is cold where we have stopped," he told his sister Sevenka. "Like many of the other women, our mother is crying to see her home in the village. We live in holes in the sand dunes. We live in caves beneath the rocky ledges. One woman walks toward Oraibi each day and stands looking, looking, looking, just to see the smoke rising from the chimney pots. Many hearts are filled with hate because we have been torn from our houses and our corn rooms where our harvest was stored. We know most of the corn has been taken, still we would be glad for the little we could carry away."

So Oraibi lost its heart. The banished ones sorrowed on the mesa to the west—sorrowed and suffered through a cold, long winter, and were still further divided when one faction, torn between returning to follow Tawaquaptewa or remaining with

Yeokeoma, moved to a site about a mile from Hotevilla and established Bakabi.

Added to that was the distress caused by the arrival of troops who arrested Yeokeoma and most of the younger men of the new village and sent them away to prison because of the trouble at Oraibi and their resistance to governmental authority.

Tawaquaptewa was also arrested, but was sent to Sherman Institute, the Indian school at Riverside, California. Before he left Oraibi, he and his followers celebrated their so-called victory by giving a Butterfly Dance.

Polingaysi was one of the dancers. Small and agile, with rhythm in her heart, she danced the dainty and intricate steps with delight, too thrilled by the performance to be saddened by the event it celebrated. It was the first and last time she took part in the traditional dances of the Hopis.

Yeokeoma had already served one term in prison for resisting the government, but he told his friend Qoyawayma that he would be punished four times. After the fourth time, he predicted, he would be left alone to die in peace.

Polingaysi remembered the fourth imprisonment. The old man was jailed at the Agency at Keams Canyon. One of his relatives asked Matthew, Polingaysi's brother, to take the old man some *piki* when he went to the Agency.

"Yeokeoma was in the basement, locked in," Matthew told his family later. "He was busy weaving. Another man, one of his friends, was making a pair of moccasins. They were working and talking. Just waiting peacefully to be let out. I said, 'I have brought you some *piki*.' For a little while Yeokeoma looked sad. He looked lonesome. But he was glad to get the *piki*."

Fatalism was ingrained in Yeokeoma, as it is in all Hopis. He accepted the ill fortune that had overtaken him as something that could not be averted. It was to be, therefore he must endure it. When he was released he returned to his people as strongly determined as ever to live out his life in the Hopi pattern. There was no changing him. He was devoted to his principles. He would die for them if that became necessary, but he would not discard them for the white man's way. Others might travel the trail of the *Bahana,* might try to be part white and part Hopi, but he would never yield. And only in the face of his strenuous objection would any of the young people of his village step out into the white man's world.

It was not immediately apparent that Oraibi had been torn apart on the day of the struggle. For a time dances were conducted as usual, but Oraibi had been depleted of the clansmen necessary for observance of some of the rituals.

A sad factor of the episode was that it was foreknown to both Bear and Spider Clan chieftains.

"What would you say caused the split in 1906?" a Bear Clan man was asked some years later.

The man thought about it for a long interval, then said: "That was planned from the beginning. Spider Clan knew that he could not live long with other leaders. That's why he made the mark on the rock north of the village." He referred to the line Yeokeoma had drawn and over which he was pushed.

"Were you at Oraibi at the time?"

"You mean when they *na-hon-a-ya?* When the people parted? No. I left the village before it happened. I knew it would take place soon."

"How did you know this?"

"Spider Clan leader came to our house twice. The first time he said, 'I ask you Bear Clan people to let me and my people leave you. There will be enough of other clans to take care of you in the ceremonials. We can no longer live here under changing conditions. We want to live as Hopi people.' "

"What did your people say?"

"Nothing. Next time he demanded to be let go, but he said,

'There is to be no blood spilled at the parting, for it will mean separation, brother from brother. I want my people to live.' Then I got mad."

"Why? Wasn't it right that he should want his people to live?"

"Yes. But it was known from the beginning that this parting was to be. There was to be no Spider Clan left, because they were said to be tricky, unmerciful, and wicked. They were to be wiped from the earth, like the wicked people who escaped when we Hopis came from the Underworld in the beginning."

Bear Clan lost face by the break in the Hopi ranks. Ancient leaders of Oraibi and Hopiland, they had gone against everything they had been taught since childhood. Against peacefulness, against angering the spirits of others. They had committed sins that they could not spit out over their shoulders at prayer time. Now they could not conscientiously sit before Father Sun in meditation, nor could they heal their hurts with the rays of the rising sun. The hurts were too deep.

Polingaysi's parents began to feel uneasy on the mesa. Perhaps they felt they should be with the conservatives, suffering in their new homesite to the west. Perhaps it was the missionaries who interested them in leaving the ancient village and building a dwelling below the cliffs at Kiakotsmovi—New Oraibi—where the government had built the school. At any rate, Fred Qoyawayma selected acreage for himself and his children and constructed a stone house in New Oraibi.

Old Oraibi began to dwindle in population. More and more families followed the example of the Qoyawaymas, and the stone houses of Old Oraibi slowly emptied.

FOUR

TAWAQUAPTEWA was right. Polingaysi had wanted to be a white man. The white man had abundant supplies of food, good clothing, and opportunities to travel. She had a desire to share the good things of the white way of living.

It was soon after the Oraibi split, and before the Qoyawayma family moved into the New Oraibi home, that Polingaysi heard of plans for sending a group of Hopi young people to Riverside for training at Sherman Institute. She began to daydream of going with them. She envied the chosen ones. Why, she asked herself, shouldn't she be asked to go along? Hadn't she been a good scholar? Hadn't she learned to spell words, and write them, and speak them, at least after a fashion? She was ready for a taste of life beyond the mesas.

She was old enough to be included in the group that was going to that far-off place beyond the Snowy Peaks. Although she was so small that she might well be mistaken for a ten-year-old, she was in reality in her early teens, perhaps fourteen. But, as far as worldliness was concerned, she was completely ignorant.

One clear day in that September of 1906, she saw a covered wagon on the hill road that led down from Second Mesa. A vast excitement ran through her. Perhaps this wagon had in it the children from Keams Canyon school, the children who were bound for the outside world of the white man.

Stationing herself at a vantage point, she waited for the wagon's arrival in the village. It could be that the wagon contained relatives or friends, though no ceremonial dances were being held at that time. Relatives were always received with fitting honors. One of the uncles would take them in tow and go with them from house to house, introducing them to other relatives. At each place they would eat a little *piki,* some sweet corn cakes, or other food given to them in welcome.

But these people in the wagon that rolled steadily nearer, drawn by a lazy team of horses, were not relatives. Boys scrambled from the canvas-covered enclosure and came running ahead, racing each other in Hopi fashion. These, Polingaysi felt certain, were children from the government school at the Agency, embarking on their great adventure. Then and there she made her decision to go with them.

As soon as the driver pulled the horses to a halt near the trading post, Polingaysi ran to the wagon and climbed up to have a look inside. There was an Oraibi girl in the wagon, and to that familiar, friendly face Polingaysi appealed for information.

"Are you coming home to stay, or are you going on somewhere in this wagon?" she asked.

"We're going to the land of oranges," the schoolgirl told her. "Far away. In California."

Polingaysi's face took on a rapt expression. Land of oranges! She visualized ground covered with great, golden oranges, sweet to the taste, pungent to the nostrils. How wonderful it would be to live in such a land! Still, perhaps there was a trick in this. Would those children ever be allowed to return to the mesas?

She plied the other girl with questions and was somewhat reassured. They were going to a school. They would ride from Winslow on a train which would go very fast. What was a train? The girl didn't know, exactly. Someone had told her it was a string of long houses on wheels, drawn by an iron house that screamed with ear-splitting loudness. They would come home someday, but not soon.

Polingaysi eyed the girl suspiciously. Was she telling the truth? Was there such a place as she described? And how did she know about the thing that screamed, since she had never seen it?

Another of the girls, a few years older, took the doubt from Polingaysi's eyes. Their teacher had shown them pictures of trains. She had also shown them pictures of orange trees, heavy with fruit, this girl said, like peaches on the Hopi peach trees, only much larger.

Polingaysi relinquished her picture of oranges golden on the ground, accepted a picture of orange trees.

"There are so many the schoolchildren play ball with them," one of the boys said. "Anyone may eat as many as he wishes. There are piles of them."

Polingaysi abruptly jumped to the ground and sped homeward. Arriving breathless and windblown, she asked her mother to teach her to make a plaque.

Astonished, her mother asked why she was suddenly in such a hurry to learn an art she had never before been willing to consider. Hopi girls from time immemorial had learned to make reed and yucca plaques as a matter of course. One of the duties of a Hopi mother is to teach her daughters plaque-making, for many plaques are needed in a Hopi household. Anna had been an apt and willing student. Polingaysi had been too restless, too filled with projects of another nature to learn such sedentary work.

"I want to buy an orange," Polingaysi answered truthfully. "The trader will give me oranges for the plaque. I tasted an orange once, but I don't remember very well how it tasted. I think it tasted very good. If oranges taste good, I'm going to the land of oranges where the other schoolchildren are going." She had already picked up a plaque her mother had nearly completed. "I will finish this one. I am in a hurry," she told her mother.

"Always you must be doing something different," her mother sighed. "How is it that you are not content to be a true Hopi, but must learn more and more of the ways of the *Bahana?* Where is this land? Who is going, and why?"

Bent over her work, Polingaysi told about the wagon and the children from Keams Canyon school.

"I have heard of this school in the west," Sevenka said. "Your father told me. Children from many Indian tribes go there. Even Foreheads."

For an instant Polingaysi's hands were still. Foreheads. Would it be safe? But then, there would be teachers to protect her from the Navajos.

Her mother sat down beside her and began instructing her in plaque-making.

"I am glad to see that you are interested in this work," she said, "but as for going away with anyone, that you cannot do. You are too young to be away from home. You belong here, with me and your father."

Polingaysi did not argue. She finished the plaque, not too skillfully, and took it to the store. The oranges she received for it tasted sweet and tangy. She decided to eat many of them in California. Going to the home of her California-bound friend, she asked when the group expected to begin the journey.

The student gave her bad news. There would be no traveling until the parents had signed a paper stating their willingness to allow their children to go away to school. Some of the parents were too conservative to want their children to leave them. The sparkle of excitement died from Polingaysi's eyes. Would her parents sign for her? She doubted it. Should she try to find a way to go, or should she stay at home and become the true Hopi maiden her parents wished her to be?

She had to think this over. Down the path there was a huge

boulder that had broken from the cliff and fallen against another rock in such a manner as to provide a hiding place. In this sheltered nook Polingaysi sat down to think. A broken bit of pottery lay at her feet, and from long habit she picked it up and began digging in the sand with it.

She thought of the wagon leaving Oraibi without her. She thought of the other girls and boys waving goodbye. She visualized their happy time in the land of oranges while she languished here at home. Tossing the potsherd aside she returned home to ask permission to go with the others to Riverside. Her parents flatly refused to allow her to go.

Polingaysi brooded and waited, keeping in touch with her more fortunate friend. The night before the travelers were to begin their journey by covered wagon to the railroad town of Winslow, about seventy miles south of Oraibi, Polingaysi made a bundle of her few belongings and hid it beside the house. Before daylight she crept out, snatched up her bundle, and fled.

No one was near the covered wagon. She climbed into it and crouched beneath the wagon seat, hoping no one would discover her until it was too late to force her return to the village. She had slept fitfully the night before, and it was chilly in the pre-dawn. She pulled her blanket around her and fell asleep, to be awakened by the driver, a white man.

"Well, now! What's this? You a stowaway?" he laughed.

"No." Polingaysi shook her head, not knowing what the word meant. "I'm going to the land of oranges. I came early to keep you from waiting for me."

Then he asked her for "the paper" and she had no paper. He told her he couldn't take her without her parents' consent and asked her to get out of the wagon. Her hopes were dwindling, but she sat there stubbornly. She would not surrender to circumstance, though she did not know what to do next.

The driver summoned a Hopi girl who was acting as overseer of the girl students, and this girl told Polingaysi she must get out of the wagon.

"You're too young," she said. "You'd be lonesome. You'd be crying for your parents before we got to Winslow."

"I am old enough not to cry," Polingaysi insisted, her eyes flashing proudly. "I will not get out of the wagon. I am going along."

The girl went away and returned with Polingaysi's parents. Sevenka, large and stern always, seemed even more imposing to the defiant girl in the wagon box, but Polingaysi's slender little father wore a look of understanding on his expressive face.

"I think we should allow her to go," he told his wife. "She will be well taken care of. She will learn more of the writing marks that are in books. I think we should sign the paper."

Sevenka gave in. "It shall be as you say," she said turning away to hide the tears in her eyes.

Thus Polingaysi won her weaponless battle for another sample of white man's education.

Before the wagon left the village her father came to tell her goodbye and to place in her hand three silver dollars, his wage for six days of hard labor for the missionary. Polingaysi had never before seen so much money at one time. Awed, she knotted the silver pieces into a corner of her shawl and held the knot tightly in one hand, fearful of losing her fortune.

How wealthy she felt! As the wagon rolled away from her home, from parents, brothers, sisters, and grandparents, her mind teemed with plans for spending the money. What a lot of things she could buy with it!

The long trip across the desert that day was like a party. The children got out now and then and walked to stretch their legs. They played games whenever the horses rested. But that night, in camp on the bank of the Little Colorado, the world seemed cold and unfriendly.

Coyotes howled, sending shivers of apprehension over Polingaysi. She rolled up in a blanket, as did the others, but could not go to sleep at once. Instead, she thought of her patient mother, her adoring and adorable brothers, Anna and her new baby boy. In spite of her determination, tears oozed beneath her eyelids, but she smothered her loneliness and no one knew she wept. Once it flashed into her mind to slip away and return to the village, following the wagon tracks. She could make the trip in two days, or at most three. Then she thought of her mother. She could almost see the accusing black eyes and hear the stern words: "Finish what you begin. Those who leave things half done get boils on their heads. Do you want boils on your head?"

In the quiet dark, Polingaysi's fingers crept up to her scalp. Her exploring fingers found no evidence of boils forming there. It was best not to take a chance of getting them. Her mother would scorn her, if she went back weeping and sniveling, a coward running away from her own decision.

Again, there was no turning back.

It was the first time Polingaysi had ever slept away from home. She had once more willfully departed from the Hopi frame of action. Whatever happened to her was her own fault; it would be up to her to take the consequences without complaint.

The realization that they were indeed leaving their desert home seemed to strike the older students the next morning. They were tired, silent, awed by the change, even before they reached Winslow.

After their pueblo villages, crowded together on the mesas' rocky points, the small town of Winslow seemed to them a noisy and huge place. Trains rumbled and screeched along the rails that bisected the town, accompanied by a clickety-clacking sound, unfamiliar yet interesting. The streets seemed alive with men and women; freight wagons, buggies, buckboards formed a traffic pattern along the main street. Cowboys and Navajos on horseback turned to stare at the wild-looking little band from the mesas.

For the first time, Polingaysi entered a store where quantities of food, dress goods, and other supplies were displayed. Why they went inside, she could never remember. Perhaps the white matron in charge of the girls merely wanted them to see the interior of a normal place of business in the white man's world. Certainly they were not a clean group of young people. Wearing their worn ticking dresses, cheap shoes, Hopi shoulder blankets, and trading-post shawls, the girls were less than charming. The boys were just as unkempt in their homemade floursack shirts and denim pants, and just as shy and frightened as the girls.

That night they slept in a warehouse, with the government matron in charge. Next day they were herded onto a passenger train to begin their journey by rail to Riverside, California. Never had Polingaysi heard such a confusing din. Never had she imagined so much movement and clanking of machinery as followed. Then the train pulled out of the station, wheezing and whistling and clickety-clacking up the grade.

Polingaysi sat stiffly on the red plush cushion beside another girl and stared at the changing scenery. The desert growth changed from rabbit brush to low junipers and pinyons and, as the train carried its passengers into higher elevations, ponderosa pines appeared, rosy-boled and green of foliage. One of the boys was the first to spy the snowy heights of the San Francisco Peaks that tower above the town of Flagstaff.

"Look!" he whispered, indicating the direction by pursing his lips and pointing with his chin. "Nu-va-da-ka-o-vi!"

Polingaysi went with the others to the north side of the car and stared at the beautiful peaks. She had known them all her life, but this was her first close look at them. On those jagged peaks, according to Hopi legend, lived the Kachina people, ancestors of her father.

56

"Remember, you are a child of the Kachinas," her paternal grandmother had always told her. Hopis must not boast, they must not show pride, but they could feel inner pride in ancestry. Her father was of Kachina Clan, therefore she was a child of the Kachinas, as a daughter of a Bow Clan man would be a child of the Bow people. To Polingaysi, identification with the august, revered, legendary Kachinas was a mark of distinction.

While the children stared, a man came through the coach selling fruit. Polingaysi forgot the mountains. Should she spend a portion of her fortune for food? There were apples and oranges in the basket. With those she was familiar, but what were those long, yellow things that grew in a bunch like so many fat fingers?

A married couple had been assigned to the coach with the younger children. Both were very young and eager to go to school in California. Polingaysi asked the young wife about the fruit. She giggled, hiding her face as she admitted her own ignorance, but her husband knew.

"Bananas," he said. "Good to eat, but very sweet. I do not like them very much."

Polingaysi, the adventurous, decided to try one. She also bought an apple and an orange, then was horrified to see how much of her silver dollar she had spent. Her chagrin increased when, after peeling the banana as the young man instructed, she was repelled by the strange taste and texture of the fruit. She gave the rest of it away, smarting under the knowledge that she had acted foolishly and without due consideration.

"I'll not spend any more of my money until I get to the land of oranges," she vowed silently, and kept her vow. When tempted to break it, she remembered her mother's remedy for hunger and drank a cup of water to "weigh her down."

Arriving in Riverside in a stupor of weariness, the nervous and frightened strangers were taken to dormitories. Polingaysi, the youngest and smallest, was assigned to a place in one of the dormitories for girls and told to remove her clothing and take a shower.

Now this was terror, genuine terror, from the viewpoint of a Hopi maiden. Who could tell from what spring this gushing water came? Who knew, positively, that Water Serpent was not peering from that faucet?

The fear of snakes had been instilled in Polingaysi at a very early age. Her first awareness of the dreaded water serpent came when she was little more than a baby. Toddling after her mother, her own little water jar on her back, she had gone to the village spring. At that time it was like a huge cone, narrowing at the bottom where there was a pool of water that reflected the blue sky and brightly colored cliffs. The steep sides were terraced, and the women often spent hours there, gossiping while they awaited their turn to fill their jars.

As children will, Polingaysi absorbed everything and asked many questions. At the spring's edge, Polingaysi's mother caught her handwoven woolen blanket dress closely about her legs as she bent to dip water into her *wigoro*. Across from them, where the water seeped from the mossy rocks, there was an earthen pot. In that light it looked very pretty to the little girl. Above it something moved. It was a feather, affixed to a prayer stick which was thrust into a little niche above the water and the submerged pot.

"Look, Mother," Polingaysi said. "Someone has lost a pretty little pot."

Her mother almost fell into the water, so violent was her reaction.

"Don't look back in there, and don't talk," she hissed. "Do you want to be charmed by Water Serpent?"

Her mother's stern and fearful face, and the haste with which she filled her water jar and hurried out of the funnel of the spring, was enough to impress the episode upon the child. Later she learned that the reason women held their skirts about them at the spring was to guard against molestation by the snake, which might make a girl or woman become pregnant, just by breathing on her. Also, that the little pot she had admired was a "transplanter" buried there by some priest of the rainmakers, and therefore sacred. To have removed it would have been dangerous.

And here, in this strange room, she was being asked to bare her body and stand beneath that stream of water, to be seen and perhaps breathed upon by Water Serpent.

The matron in charge was unaware of Polingaysi's fears. She might have been more tolerant had she known why the girl cowered in a corner, her eyes wide with fright. As it was, she made it clear that Polingaysi was to take her shower . . . at once!

That night for the first time, Polingaysi slept in a real bed. She climbed up onto it giddy with fear and nervousness, feeling the softness of the mattress and the resilience of the springs beneath the tautly drawn sheets. Her bed was one of many, ranged the length of the room. In each bed there was a girl, a stranger, not one of them a Hopi from Polingaysi's homeland. Eyes watched her get into bed and lay her freshly washed head on the white pillow, but no one spoke a word of welcome and no one smiled. They were strangers, not knowing nor caring how this new girl felt. For all the comfort they offered, the Oraibian might as well have been alone.

She had no sooner pulled up the covers than helpless tears began to flow. She tried to blink them back, but they kept coming, gushing like a spring from beneath her closed eyelids. Finally she dived beneath the pillow and wept, all but suffocating before her tears were spent.

For weeks, each night was a repetition of the first. With the coming of darkness, all the confusions of the day welled up in her and had to be released.

Riverside. Land of oranges. Land of perfume. Time of torture. After more than half a century, Polingaysi still could not recall that interval without a surge of emotion, remembering the white nights filled with the cloying scent of the orange and lemon groves, remembering the stifled sobbing of the lonely child she had been.

But there was another, happier, memory of that time. Each day the schoolchildren sang. Song was Polingaysi's salvation.

Sevenka, Polingaysi's mother, had a strong, lovely voice and Polingaysi had inherited some of her ability. Sevenka belonged to the women's society called the Mazhrau; a dancing and singing group. She composed songs regularly for her own society, and at one time composed a song which was used for years afterward by the Niman Dancers in the late-July ceremony that closes the Kachina calendar for the year. This was a stepping out of her woman's place to compete with men. Sevenka's songs were songs of living prayer. Long hours of practice were required of the Mazhrau members, in order that they might learn the songs and fit them to the dance steps. They were not recorded, except in the memories of the women.

Polingaysi's voice was a sweet, high soprano, clear and true, and she had the lung power to sustain high notes. When Sevenka first noticed this, she was surprised and told the child how glad she was.

"When you were tiny," she said, "you were very ill. We thought you would not live much longer. Your sister was also ill at that time. Missionary Voth took her to care for, but your sister could not be saved. The medicine man, Apha, took care of you. Night and day he held you in his arms, treating you with his magic. And you lived, but you were puny for a long time." She smiled, remembering the puny one. "You used to run after your grandfather when he went to the fields. He had long legs and you could not keep up with him. He told me this: 'Keep that child at home. I have to stop for her, because after a while I hear her panting after me like a little lizard.' I never thought you would grow up to have such good lungs."

Polingaysi's "strong lungs" brought her to the attention of her teachers. In spite of her years of attendance at the New Oraibi day school she knew very little English and mispronounced many words, but this was unimportant. She could sing. Her voice was dependable. She could learn the words with a little effort.

She was unaware of the interest her voice had stimulated until she was singled out to take a leading part in one of the school programs. Then, with characteristic Hopi reticence, she tried to escape being spotlighted. The thought of making a mistake before an audience was horrifying. Better not to sing at all than to be embarrassed. Her teachers understood but were firm with her. Finally her innate good sense and her love of music overcame her fears. Singing was not hard, she told herself, and she would practice. She could do what they asked of her.

She began to receive pleasure from giving pleasure. Compliments encouraged her and aroused in her a desire to excel. Some of the hard knots of fear began to dissolve from her mind and float away on wings of song. She found in this activity a way to express her pent-up yearnings, her uncertainties, and her loneliness, and to rise above them.

One of her teachers began to show an especially warm interest in her. She often stopped to talk to Polingaysi and to try to engage her in conversation. One day she asked the embarrassing question: "How old are you, Bessie?"

Polingaysi looked down at her feet, admitting in a low murmur that she did not know.

"You're teasing me," her teacher said. "Tell me. When is your birthday?"

Birthday! Polingaysi looked puzzled and frightened. There were no such things within her experience. You were born. You lived.

You died. What difference did it make when these events occurred? Tears sparkling in her eyes, she looked toward one of the older teachers for help. The older woman understood.

"She probably has no idea of a birthday, as we know them. You see, Hopi mothers kept no records in her day, and few could tell you, now, on what particular day one of their children was born. Her mother may relate her birth to some ceremonial dance or village event, and so place it more or less definitely as in spring, summer, fall, or winter. We think Bessie's about fourteen."

"Oh, Bessie, I'm sorry," her new friend apologized. Once the awkward moment was over, they talked freely. The result was that Polingaysi was invited to live at the home of the teacher and her husband and help with housework.

The white couple had no children of their own, and lavished more than the usual attention on her. They might have been even more affectionate had Polingaysi not maintained her reserve, even with them. She had never worked in the kitchen of white people, but they were tolerant. They showed her how to do housework in the white man's way and taught her English in the process. She soon began to develop a well-rounded vocabulary, and this increased her confidence in her own ability. She began to emerge, ever so little and timidly, from her tight little shell of doubt.

She had her father's desire to learn, and to earn money. When her benefactors told her they were going to pay her for her work, she was overwhelmed with happiness. She who had never before had money, except for the three dollars her father had given her, was to have money of her own. She would be a person of substance yet. She didn't mind that her teacher friend was not giving her the money outright, but was placing it in a fund from which portions could be drawn out as needed.

"I will work hard," she promised, "and I will save. When I have many, many dollars I will draw it all out and," her roguish eyes twinkled, "do something big with it, like building a house!"

But there were other experiences in store for her. She had to do her share of the work at the Institute, which included scrubbing floors, doing dishes, making beds, and helping in various other departments as she was needed. The scrubbing detail was most detested. With half a dozen others, she got down on her knees each Saturday to scrub the floor of the big dining hall. A patch of floor was scrubbed, then rinsed and wiped, and another section attacked. The work was slow, and hard on the knees.

It was good that there was variety. That first fall in Riverside, Polingaysi was detailed to pick tomatoes at the Institute's Arlington farm. The children went from Riverside in a big farm wagon, enjoying the trip immensely and making a picnic of it as they did their work. There were cows at the farm, and many chickens. The mesa children stared at them, especially the cattle, unused as they were to any cattle except range stock, and they enjoyed the chickens. The cackling and crowing, the busy scratching for food, fitted in with their concept of life: dance, sing, then attend to the business of eating.

The Hopi children, including Polingaysi, seldom minded having to peel potatoes. Potatoes were as plentiful as oranges, and the children could eat as many sweet, raw potatoes as they could hold, while peeling the bucketfuls that went into the huge cauldrons to be cooked.

There was a classroom at the farm where Polingaysi learned a great deal about vegetables and fruits, as well as routine subjects such as spelling and arithmetic. Age was not important. Little ones and teenagers attended the classes and worked wherever they were assigned, enjoying the fresh air and sunshine, and satisfying their curiosity about this land of abundance. They were still following a set pattern, much as they had done on the mesas, but their field of knowledge was gradually expanding.

Polingaysi wrote home about the wagonloads of oranges, the fields of watermelons, the sweet potatoes and squash, the cheese and butter. The missionaries would read the letters to her parents. She could imagine her mother's reaction to her reference to using butter. "Putter," Sevenka called it, and eyed it with distaste, insisting that it was poisonous and good only for putting on one's face.

Polingaysi had no desire to return to Oraibi during the summer vacation period. She was learning at Riverside, and she was earning a little money which she hoarded carefully, thinking ahead to that someday when there would be enough of it for some large undertaking.

Her work in the school laundry brought her into the new adventure of sewing. She began by darning socks, her instructor being so exacting that more often than not at first, Polingaysi had to take out her stitches and begin all over.

Once that art was mastered, she went on to patching and mending, and finally to sewing new materials on the sewing machine. That gave her an idea. She had a knack for sewing; she would sew for the other girls and charge them for the work. It was a splendid idea. Her teachers were pleased with her ability to make her own clothes and encouraged the other girls to trust her with their materials. Soon she was making more than the small wage of three dollars per week.

She almost dreaded the day when her four years at Sherman would come to a close and she would return to her home. She was certain she would not like it. She had outgrown village life. She had burst like a butterfly from the confining chrysalis of her Hopi childhood.

A new mission station had been built north of the village of New Oraibi, and there were white helpers there. Another child, a little girl, had been born to Sevenka. Lydia, she had been named. She was to be the last of Sevenka's children. The older brother, Hugh, ill for so many years, had gone on into the land of spirit. Alfred, the youngest brother, was preparing to enter Sherman Institute where Homer and Matthew were enrolled.

There would be many other changes, Polingaysi knew. Many of her former girl friends had married. They would be interested now in their homes and their babies. They would want to talk about plaque designs and pottery-making. They would regale her with village gossip which no longer interested her.

Her mother would be talking to her about eligible young Hopi men and urging her to marry and settle down. But she knew she would not be happy as a pueblo wife. For all its richness and beauty, the pattern life of the Hopi no longer impressed her with its importance. She was more interested in learning new ways of living and in losing the fragments of the past that still clung to her.

Yet at times she felt a great loneliness, an undefined yearning for the security of home and parents and set patterns of behavior. How carefree her childhood had been! How sad that she could never recapture that simple freedom.

Sometimes when the fog came in from the Pacific and the scent of orange and lemon blossoms thickened, Polingaysi dreamed of Arizona, feeling the caress of the desert wind, seeing the great, uncluttered distances, the pink sand, the golden-bronze sunsets, the smiling faces of her Hopi people.

Then she would think of the ones who would laugh at her, behind their blankets. Polingaysi, the little one who wanted to be a white man. They would not want to hear about her new life. What if she could sing like a bird? What if she could cook and sew in the manner of the white man? She was no longer a true Hopi.

Blown by the winds of her own indecision, she veered from one idea to the other, needing a stabilizing influence and finding none. She almost envied the girls who looked forward to returning home and taking up the old ways of the village. They would dress a little better. They would understand more about what was going on in the outside world, but they would be content

with home and children and routine duties, with Kachina dancing as entertainment and gossip for idle hours at the village spring
below Pumpkinseed Hill.

Many times she asked herself angrily what it was she wanted.
What must she have to make her contented with life? She was
reaching out, but for what?

FIVE

ALL TOO SOON, from Polingaysi's point of view, her four years of schooling at Sherman Institute came to an end. Much though she loved her family, she did not relish the idea of going home to stay. She had made many friends in California. She had learned the white man's way of living and liked it. And she had also made great strides in the field of music.

The clothes she packed in a suitcase for the trip home were neat and new, products of her skill in sewing. A sewing machine would be one of her first purchases, she promised herself. She would make good clothes for her mother and the younger children.

Thanks to her teacher friend, she had a small nest egg in the bank, and this made the occasion less dismal. At least, she was not returning penniless. There was the promise of a future for her. With mixed emotions of apprehension and anticipation, she told her benefactor and other friends goodbye and boarded the train for Winslow where her father would meet her.

Excitement shook her when she saw the San Francisco Peaks looming against the sky. Flagstaff. Another hour of travel and she would reach Winslow.

Her father was waiting, a small figure with a red band around his black hair. He came trotting over to greet her with a smile and a word of welcome, took her luggage and led her to the wagon near the depot.

"You went away a child," he said, "you have returned a woman. Though," he added, with a sidewise glance, "you did not grow much, in spite of all that good food you wrote letters about."

There was the Little Colorado to ford, then the dirt road pointed to the pink Hopi Buttes, entrance to Hopiland. After the great gardens and luxuriant citrus groves of California, the desert distances amazed Polingaysi. So much land, so little growth.

When from miles away she saw the outlines of Third Mesa, with its straggle of houses on the rocky eminence, she felt a tug at her heartstrings. Not for herself, but for her Hopi people was she touched. They had lived in this desolation for centuries, enduring the worst the desert could dole out to them rather than leave their own land, their little rock houses, their tiny gardens in the sandy waste.

At that time—early summer—the Niman corn was waving its green leaves like banners proclaiming the unquenchable faith of Hopi farmers in the goodness of nature. Bean plants were beginning to grow in short rows protected by brush windbreaks. Farmers were at work in the fields, hardly distinguishable from the scarecrows that flapped their rags in warning to marauding birds. In the pink dunes about three miles south of the village of New Oraibi, a cottonwood tree with its feet in the sand was unfurling green leaves. Polingaysi saw it and exclaimed.

"You are right, it was not there before," her father said. "I planted it. It is good to see it putting down roots and reaching its branches upward to Rain People. It is one of many trees I have planted since I moved from the old village. I like to see trees grow. The shade is always welcome." He added thoughtfully, "To men and animals and birds."

At last they drove into the houseyard and saw Sevenka coming to meet them, the little girl, Lydia, in her arms. The younger brother was at home. The older ones were at Riverside, furthering their education as their sister had done.

Polingaysi looked at the little house and the windswept yard where chickens pecked at bits of grain. The poverty of the scene made her heartsick. This life was not for her. She would never again be happy in the old pattern. She had gone too far along the path of the white man.

Sevenka had plastered the walls and floor of the rock house in honor of Polingaysi's homecoming. Bright new plaques decorated the walls. New pottery was on the shelves. The iron cookstove, which served the family instead of the usual corner fireplace, had a pot of cornmeal bubbling on it. But there was no table, and there were no bedsteads.

Polingaysi scolded her parents.

"Why haven't you bought white man's beds to sleep on? And a table? You should not be eating on the floor as the Old Ones did. When I was a little girl I did not mind sleeping on the floor and eating from a single bowl into which everyone dipped. But I am used to another way of living now, and I do not intend to do these things."

"What shall I do with my daughter, who is now my mother?" Sevenka sighed, but Polingaysi's father attacked the problem from a practical angle. He went to someone who was building a house and got boards enough to make a crude bed. On this frame he placed a ticking bag filled with shredded cornhusks. It was a bed off the floor for this demanding, headstrong girl. Now, he would have to make a table. He could see that Polingaysi would give him no peace until this was done.

Her mother hesitantly led Polingaysi into the small storage room and lifted a cloth from a stack of beautiful plaques.

"These I have made for your wedding," she said. "You have reached that age. You must begin to think about taking a mate."

Marriage! It had not entered Polingaysi's mind. She wanted to save money. She wanted to build a house of her own someday, but she was not ready for marriage. The image of herself, down on her knees in the grinding room, laboriously reducing the blue cornmeal to fine flour for the *piki* wedding bread, was appalling to Polingaysi. So was the image of herself as a traditional Hopi bride, clad in wrapped white-deerskin footwear, big white *ovah,* and fringed fertility sash.

She was not yet willing to become a living seed pod for her Hopi people. She loved children, but was not ready to assume the role of mother.

Besides, although she had had some schoolgirl crushes, she had never been seriously attracted to any young man. Nor would she be willing to marry in traditional Hopi fashion, complete with washing of the hair and twisting of the locks of bride and groom, as her parents would expect her to do. And for no man, she told herself with spirit, would she grind corn on her knees.

With genuine sorrow she looked at the lovely plaques. She knew the hours of labor their making had cost her mother. In her childhood, Polingaysi had often helped her mother gather *sewi* stems for the plaque ribs, and rabbit brush which had to be peeled, each small stem separately, with the fingernails, before this weaving material could be dyed and used. And, as far back as she could remember, her mother had had a plaque in some stage of development.

On this first day at home she would have been glad not to hurt her mother's feelings, but this could not be. There were tears in her eyes as she slowly shook her head.

"They are not for me, Mother. Sell them. Buy food. Dishes. Clothing. There are many things you need."

"You are a woman," her mother said, her voice uncertain. "You should have a man and babies. You should have a home of your own."

"I intend to have a home of my own," Polingaysi declared. "I will build a home for myself some day. A good home."

Sevenka looked steadily into the flushed and defiant face of her daughter, and her own face was sad. Whatever it was she saw there—implacable opposition to all things Hopi, perhaps—made her turn away, weeping silently. Gently she took the white cloth in her two hands, and slowly she pulled it up over her dead hopes.

Polingaysi would not grind corn, and it annoyed her to see her mother on her knees day after day. Why, she asked Sevenka, didn't she use a machine?

Sevenka was amazed. She was strong, she said. She had ground corn into meal ever since she was a small child. It worried her that Polingaysi felt so strongly about it.

"Mother Corn has fed you, as she has fed all Hopi people, since the long, long ago when she was no larger than my thumb. Mother Corn is a promise of food and life. I grind with gratitude for the richness of our harvest, not with cross feelings of working too hard. As I kneel at my grinding stone, I bow my head in prayer, thanking the great forces for provision. I have received much. I am willing to give much in return, for as I have taught you, there must always be a giving back for what one receives." She added, in a gently chiding voice, "It is sad that the white man's way has caused you to forget the Hopi way."

Ashamed at having provoked her mother into this display of emotion, Polingaysi stood with bowed head. She knew the importance of corn to a Hopi.

"I presented you with your first Mother Corn," her grandmother had told her long ago, and she knew the symbolism of the birth ritual. A perfect ear of white corn was required. One with straight rows of kernels that grew up over the tip of the ear. The baby's own Mother Corn, presented at birth, was bathed with the child in the same water, and cradled with it during the twenty days following birth. It was presented with the child at the naming ceremony on the mesa's edge, when the new entity received its spiritual "I am, I am," with a blessing of golden pollen from the sacred corn.

For a moment the old way, with its depth of meaning, beckoned, but the new way won.

The missionaries had told Polingaysi to stop being a heathen, insisting that the superstitious rituals should be tossed off first of all. She had tried to obey. Of what benefit would it be to her to revert now to the old ways of her people? The white man's way was good. It had provided for her an education, food, clothing, white man's skills. Yes, and money in the bank—what seemed an enormous sum to Polingaysi, who had very little conception of money and its true value.

The older Hopi people were laughing at her—and ridicule cuts a Hopi to the quick. How much more would they laugh if she gave up what she had fought for and returned to village ways, just another foolish schoolgirl who couldn't stick with the white life, but had to come running home to her parents, back to the security of tribal ways.

"I haven't forgotten, Mother," she said, lifting her head. "But I have gone too far. I have set my course. As you told me the first day I went to school, there is no turning back.

"I have the Hopi reverence for corn. I respect it as our ancestral food, but sell the plaques just the same, for I'll never need them. I know you made them because of your love for me, and I thank you, Mother. *Asquali.*"

Asquali. That Hopi word for "thank you" touched the mother's tender heart.

"You are still a Hopi," she murmured. "You will not forget the pattern life of the Hopi."

Chimney pots were used as stovepipes in Old Oraibi

A Hopi woman shapes a storage jar

Polingaysi's father, Fred Qoyawayma, at Old Oraibi, as he looked
at the time of the birth of his daughter

Fred Qoyawayma with H. R. Voth at Newton, Kansas, when he
accompanied the missionary on a trip to that Mennonite community

Chief Tawaquaptewa, of Old Oraibi, who died in 1960
at the age of 106

Children of Old Oraibi, around the time of the establishment of the first school below the mesa

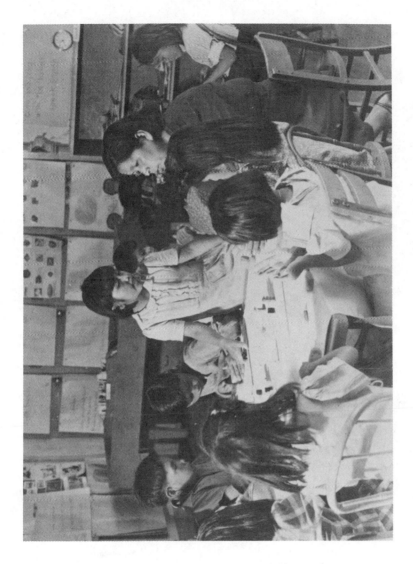

Polingaysi with the children of a later generation in her classroom at New Oraibi

A street in Old Oraibi in the early years of this century

After that, Polingaysi's parents seemed to stop trying to change her. Instead, with all the energy in her sturdy body and forceful mind, she set about changing them. She "talked" a table into the house, and with her own money bought dishes, pots, and pans from the store. Her mother preferred to use her own homemade pottery bowls and cooking pots, but she was proud of Polingaysi's generosity and showed the new kitchenware to her friends somewhat apologetically.

"I don't need them, but our daughter is trying to make white men of us," she told them.

Cooking was a point of conflict between Polingaysi and her mother. Sevenka was determined to cling to the old ways; Polingaysi was as determined to bake cakes and cook other foods for which her parents never had developed a liking. Sevenka was horrified when Polingaysi sacrificed three precious eggs to mix the sweet batter for a cake. Three eggs, stirred into a pot of cornmeal mush, would feed an entire family!

"You are as foolish as a white woman," she scolded. "How can you waste food like that?"

Polingaysi was not then wise enough to see that her lessons in home economics were wrong for her as a Hopi. Not that it was the fault of her teachers who, being white, had no conception of the true needs of Indian people. How could they know with what respect the frugal Hopi people looked upon food of all kinds? How could they know, or care to know, that even in good seasons the specter of starvation was always before the desert dwellers?

Polingaysi was especially bitter about the use of ceremonial foods, such as *pikami,* which all good Hopis prepare for serving during the Kachina dances. "Food for the Devils," some of her missionary friends called it, and in her desire to accept the white man's religion as well as his other benefits, Polingaysi agreed.

During the Homecoming Dance of that July she refused to sit at the table with her family on dance day.

"I will not eat food sacrificed to the Devil," she declared stiffly, denying herself food of which she was really fond.

Her mother looked sadly at Polingaysi's father. Helplessly, he shook his head. They wished to avoid wounding Polingaysi's spirit, for to offend it would be to open cracks in their own beings through which evil might enter. But they did not like her imposing upon them her strange white man's beliefs. Their only recourse was to avoid her as much as possible, allowing her to go her own way unopposed.

Gradually, Polingaysi became almost a stranger within her own home. Village women, dropping in for a chat with Sevenka, sidled past the proud Polingaysi and spoke in whispers to her mother.

She was peeling apples for a pie one day when a neighbor came in. Aware of the guest's inquisitive glances but determined not to be annoyed by them, she went on with her work. She had sliced the peeled apples into the rich crust, and was dumping the peelings and apple cores into a bucket to be thrown out to the chickens, when the neighbor whispered to her mother, "What is it your daughter makes?"

"She makes the white man's pie," Sevenka whispered back.

"But why does she put the good peelings in the scrap pail?"

"She throws them away." Sevenka's voice was sad and half a sigh.

"Throws them away!" The neighbor was stricken into brief silence. Then, "Why?"

"She is being a white man. It is their way to waste food, you know."

"*Is-u-dee!*" the neighbor exclaimed. "How shameful. Those good, sweet peelings. Those fat, black seeds in the cores. Is there nothing you can do to change her wasteful ways?"

"No. There is nothing," Sevenka said, voice heavy with resignation.

Polingaysi had not been home very long before she began to be restless and unhappy. Her cooking prowess was unappreciated. More often than not she was the only one who cared to eat the fancy pies and cakes she baked.

As for her religious views, her mother only faintly understood her lectures and had not, at that time, developed any desire to become a convert to Christianity. Her father had more insight, thanks to his long association with the Reverend Voth, but he loved the Hopi ways, the colorful Kachina dances and the Hopi ideals.

Polingaysi faced her future. The ultimate tragedy would be to be forced to slip back into the traditional Hopi village life, but as it was she was achieving nothing, standing still, and making herself and her parents miserable meanwhile.

The Voths no longer lived across Oraibi Wash, but the Reverend Jacob Frey and his family, also of the Mennonite faith, had taken over the mission work. They lived at Moenkopi, about forty miles away. Fred Qoyawayma made a trip to their home and confided his problem to Jacob Frey. The Freys were sympathetic. They offered a solution: let Polingaysi come to them, live in their home, help with cooking and housework, and in return continue to study under their tutelage, this study to include religion, as well as other subjects.

Polingaysi was grateful to her father. For the first time she realized that he had a good brain as well as clever hands. He thought a problem through, then acted upon whatever guidance he received. In a sense, he was more worldly than other Hopi men. He had not only been privileged to work and talk with the Reverend Voth and Mrs. Voth, but he had made a trip with Voth to Kansas and had seen a little of the white man's world. He had a better idea of the discontent of his active daughter, and its basis, than his village-bound wife would ever have.

Again life seemed to be opening out before the Hopi girl, Polingaysi. She looked forward eagerly to living with the Freys.

SIX

Polingaysi packed her meager belongings and placed them in the rattletrap wagon to which her father had hitched his pair of rough-coated desert horses. But before they set out for the Freys, father and daughter walked, at the father's suggestion, across the field near their home.

"You talk much about building a house of your own," Polingaysi's father said. "I want you to know, before you leave us again, that there is room on my land for all my children. I will continue to plant my crops here until you are ready to build, but you may have this plot of land, if you like the location."

The site he indicated was about two blocks from his rock house, as a white man would measure the distance. A low, sandy hill rose to the west. The land sloped gradually to the east. Oraibi Wash was about a half-mile away, and on the other side of the wash, across a generous stretch of desert land on which there were a few gardens, the great mesa Polingaysi called Dawaki—Sun Point—was a massive backdrop crowned with ranks of juniper trees.

She had visited the mesa top with a group of other children a long time before and remembered the remains of stone-walled houses that told their silent story of a prehistoric Pueblo people who had lived there for many years. There were, she remembered, great quantities of broken pottery over which the ever-shifting desert sand moved, slowly scouring them. She had been interested in the designs on the potsherds, and the quality of the baked clay.

Beyond the sand dunes with their lone cottonwood and the even line of the low buttes, rose the dark blue of buttes that seemed to mark the extreme southern distances of Hopiland. The San Francisco Peaks dominated the southwestern skyline. Beyond a young orchard of apple and peach trees, beyond the rise of the sandy hill, were village houses, with the old village of Oraibi on the mesa above. Yellow Pumpkinseed Hill thrust its bright cliffs into the northern portion of the village beyond the trading post.

Polingaysi turned slowly, noting the nearby story-and-a-half stone home of Anna and Charles and their growing brood of youngsters. They would be neighbors. She merely glanced at the disintegrating village on the mesa. She had left Old Oraibi behind her when she went to Riverside. Let it stay behind her.

In front of her, as she faced east, there was a tree. A slender young cottonwood, daintily shaking out its lacy summer leaves. It was the tree that held her attention and gave her a sense of permanence. Here she would put down roots, too. She would grow with the tree, resting in its shade, listening to the music of the wind in its branches, watching the wild birds build their nests and feed their young.

"I like this place," she told her father. "This is where I shall build my house. Here beside the tree you planted."

Now she had a building site and a goal. As soon as there was money enough in her savings account, she would begin.

On one of Polingaysi's brief visits home she had met the Reverend Frey and his wife. The Reverend Frey had come to Oraibi to study the Hopi language under the Reverend H. R. Voth, whose deep interest in the Hopi nation and their cultural background had won him national distinction in archeological and anthropological circles, as well as the hatred of many of the more conservative Hopis.

Both Mr. and Mrs. Frey were of German extraction, fair-skinned, blue-eyed, light-haired, and possessed of a quiet kindness of manner. Polingaysi remembered Mrs. Frey as a beautiful young woman, and the missionary as a tall, slender, thin-faced scholarly man with firm features and a prominent nose. When they came out to meet her and her father on their arrival at Moenkopi, she found them very little changed. A little older, that was all.

Their home, built on a terraced hillside, was well furnished and orderly. Their three children were friendly. Immediately, Polingaysi was made to feel not only that she was welcome, but that she belonged there with the Frey family, as a part of it.

She had been torturing herself with questions. Did she belong in the white man's world, or should she try to cast aside her learning and return to the easy old ways? Insecure in spite of her progress in school, she wavered unhappily between her two worlds, never seeming to belong entirely to either. The attitude of the Freys left her no questions.

"Now you are one of us, a part of our family. You may be one of our children, just as Theodore, Salina, and Wilbur are our children, and you may call us Mother Frey and Father Frey, if you will," Mrs. Frey told her.

Polingaysi felt a great welling up of love in her heart for the generous missionaries.

"I will," she said. "Oh, I will."

They were big-hearted people. They gave her the same understanding love and firm discipline that they gave their own children. Mrs. Frey never asked anything of Polingaysi that she would not expect from her own daughter. The Reverend Frey never forgot to bring home from Flagstaff or Winslow gifts for the Hopi girl as well as for his own children.

They changed her name from Bessie to Elizabeth Ruth, to the confusion of her Hopi friends and relatives. One of her aunts, asked how Bessie was getting along at Moenkopi, said uncertainly, "Bessie? It seems like she is happy there, but they don't calling her Bessie no more."

"Oh? What do they call her now?"

"I think," said the aunt, solemnly bewildered, "they calling her Liss-a-bessie, now."

The Reverend Frey was a Kansas farm lad turned missionary. A student of Greek and Hebrew, he had a brilliant and versatile mind and was able to cope with many problems, from farming and building to psychology and medicine. Like the Reverend Voth, he had learned to speak the Hopi language fluently.

The Hopi people were not at first disposed to be friendly with the Freys. This was due in part to their unfortunate experience with the Spanish priests' attempt to convert the pueblo dwellers to Catholicism, but largely because they still smarted under the methods of the Reverend Voth, who had delved into their most esoteric rituals and made his findings public.

The Hopis had refused to give any of their good land for a mission site and had, instead, grudgingly allowed the Freys to build on a hillside on which, so they thought, nothing could be grown.

They had not taken into account the Reverend Frey's talent for farming. This man recognized no difficulties in doing the Lord's work. Cheerfully he terraced the rocky hillside, piped water from a spring, irrigated his small plot, and raised crops as good as those of the Hopi farmers near him.

They watched his garden grow, concealing their admiration though they were impressed by his skill. Often Hopi farmers with mental, spiritual, or practical problems used the gardens as an excuse to walk up the hill and talk to the friendly missionary.

In those early days the Reverend Frey made his trips over the reservation in a farm wagon over which he had affixed wagon bows and a white canvas cover. Always, in season, he carried with him on these excursions gifts of vegetables from his garden—a symbolic sharing of food with the brown-skinned people he had come to serve. Mrs. Frey shared her delicious and fragrant loaves of fresh bread with the village housewives, and fed all who came to the mission hungry—and there were many.

The Freys were kind and they were honest, but their very goodness was a thorn in the flesh of a certain element in the village of Moenkopi. Tales were spread that had no foundation in fact, and many of the people the Freys had helped turned against them.

The Freys were trying, in their gentle way, to exploit them, these undermining Hopis said. Watch out for them. They were two-hearts. They might even turn out to be witches, pretending to do good. Didn't the Reverend Frey go about giving medicine to some of the people, and didn't some of those people die?

Polingaysi had relatives in the village—an uncle, several cousins. They repeated the tales they had heard about the Freys, half convinced they were true and wondering what Polingaysi would say about them. The injustice of it was enough to throw her into a fury and her denials of the vicious tales were heated. She never failed to return to the mission boiling with anger because the Freys would do nothing to squelch such gossiping. They were persecuting the Freys, those tale-spreading Hopis, and should be punished for it.

The Reverend Frey always heard her out with grave courtesy, and when she had stopped lecturing him for allowing himself to be lied about, he would assure her, smiling, his blue eyes twinkling, that he was not the judge of those people, that a lie was not the truth and mouthing it could not make it more nor less than the lie it was. Leave them to God, he advised the bristling young champion. Let God judge them in His own good time.

The current of animosity became a ferment that developed into a plot against the life of the missionary. A group of the men met and agreed that Frey should be waylaid, lassoed, and dragged to death.

Now Polingaysi and village friends of the Freys became terrified. A delegation came to the Reverend Frey, begging him to leave Moenkopi before something terrible happened to him. He heard them sadly, but was not swayed by their fear. Calmly, he assured them that his trust was in God. If this thing was to be, it was to be. He was not afraid of the outcome.

It was not long until the attempt was made. The Reverend Frey was walking past the schoolhouse when a rider came thundering along the road, twirling a lariat in one hand. The missionary saw him, but made no effort to run away. The loop was thrown, but fell short. The rider rode on, the rope trailing.

Friendly Hopis rushed to the side of the missionary and no second attempt was made. The incident would have gone unreported except for one of the Hopi friends. The culprit was apprehended and brought up for trial, and he would have been imprisoned had not the missionary made a plea for his release, declaring that the man had learned his lesson and would not repeat his error.

"He walked with God and he talked with God."

The words of the old hymn came to Polingaysi's mind as she thought of the Freys and their life in Moenkopi. There on the sunburned mesa, with the ruins of Old Oraibi holding up their empty rooms like cups crying to be filled once more with life, she hummed the song.

More than once during her life with the Freys, she had heard the Reverend Frey talking with God. Sometimes in the night, hearing his voice, she had looked out and had seen him walking the mission courtyard, bent a little forward, his hands clasped behind him, as he placed his problems in the hands of the Lord. Always on those nights, he had asked for the welfare of the Hopi people. He loved them. More than they ever knew, he loved them.

Knowing how hard he worked, in the garden, in the mission field, in his study where he was translating hymns into Hopi for his congregation, Polingaysi wished he would go to bed instead of wasting time on those stubborn Hopis. How, she asked herself, blinking back angry tears, could any *Bahana* love them so much? Why did he care what happened to them?

Frey's ministry was first and last a practical one. Never except on one momentous occasion did Polingaysi see him resort to the dramatic in his teaching. That was the day that he went through the village wearing dark glasses and carrying a lantern with a smoked chimney, its light barely visible through the blackened glass.

The Hopi people, filled with thoughts of the supernatural, watched him apprehensively.

"Duwe-Bahana—White Man Who Lives on the Terrace—has gone crazy," they whispered to each other, "or maybe he has been bewitched." And they were fearful, yet could not quite believe this misfortune had overtaken their good friend.

The Reverend Frey made no attempt to talk to them. He completed the trip around the village quietly and returned home. He knew his Hopi people. He was willing to wait until their curiosity got the better of them. That evening they began dropping in, one by one, on various pretexts. The Reverend Frey told Polingaysi to show them into his study, that he might talk with them. She was puzzled and resentful, knowing they were there to satisfy their own curiosity, but she did as she was told.

Most of the callers eventually asked, "Why did you carry a

lighted lantern while the sun was shining? And why, if you needed a lantern to help you find your way, did you cover your eyes with black glasses?"

"I was searching for the light," the Reverend Frey told them. "As you know, man has starlight to guide him. He has lantern light for dark nights when the stars hide behind clouds. He has moonlight. Yet all these guiding lights are feeble in comparison with sunlight. The sun is good. Its light is powerful. It is a light by day for mankind. But there is another light that is not seen with the eyes because it shines in men's souls. That is the light of Spirit. The light that guides us along our spiritual paths. I was searching for that light."

That little sermon touched the people of the village as no sermon preached from a pulpit could have done. It was told and retold that night and for months to come.

Like many converts to a new religion, Polingaysi was overly zealous. She was young, she was courageous, she was brash—brash enough to challenge her Hopi elders and the whole beautifully interwoven cultural pattern of Hopi life. Had she at that time been able to do so, she would have abolished all the age-old rites, the kiva rituals, the sprinkling of sacred cornmeal, and especially the making of *pahos,* or prayer sticks.

At the same time, tempering her radical approach, she had a deep and unsatisfied curiosity concerning the very things that aroused in her the strongest resentment. As she walked across the field one day after visiting her family at New Oraibi, she saw a *paho* thrust into the sand on a little hillock, its single eagle feather fluttering at the end of a short length of white cotton string.

Prayer sticks, either the long, wandlike ones with many feathers tied to them, or the short, sharpened sticks called *pahos,* are held in reverence by the Hopi people. For four days after the "planting" of a prayer, these sticks are thought to possess the essence of the offered prayer and to be very powerful and sacred. To disturb one before it has lost its power is to court disaster. Accident, even death, Polingaysi had been taught, might result.

Well known to her was the story of the white woman who took prayer sticks from a shrine, then fell and broke her leg. Behind this accident the Hopi people saw the work of the invisible forces. The spirits had resented her action and had tripped her, they were convinced.

As she bent to pull the *paho* from the sand, Polingaysi felt a wave of superstitious fear sweep over her. But she was a Christian now, she reminded herself, and need not fear the magic in a stick with a feather on it. Defiantly, she carried it home and challenged her father with it.

"What does this stick mean to you and to the Hopi people?" she asked with more arrogance than she realized. "To me, pah! It means nothing. It has no power. It's just a stick with a bit of corn-husk and a feather attached to it. Why do you, in this day and age, when you can have the message of the Bible, still have faith in sticks and feathers?"

Her father, true Hopi that he was, recoiled from the proffered *paho,* refusing to touch it. There was a worried look in his eyes.

"Must you know?" he asked.

"Of course, I must know," Polingaysi declared. "Why shouldn't I know?"

"Lay it on the table," her father said, "and I will tell you."

She placed the stick on the rough board table which she had goaded the little man into making, and the two of them bent over it.

"Do you see that blue-green, chipped-off place here at the top?" her father asked, pointing. "That is the face of the prayer stick. It represents mossy places, moisture. Now this below is the body of the prayer stick. A red color, as you can see, like our colored sand. That represents the earth. Moisture to the earth, then, is what the *paho* is for."

"A prayer for rain?"

"That, yes, and more. The stick carries a bundle on its back."

"The bit of cornhusk, bound with string? What is it for? What does it mean?"

"I don't know what is bound up in the cornhusk," her father said, "and I won't open it to find out. However, I think you might find there some grass seeds, a pinch of cornmeal, a pinch of pollen, and a drop of honey."

"But, why, why?" Polingaysi demanded impatiently. "What good does it do?"

The little Hopi man had been carving a Kachina doll from the dried root of a cottonwood. He turned away and went back to his work, sitting down crosslegged on the floor and picking up his knife and the unfinished doll. Polingaysi stood looking down at him, waiting for his answer. He thought before he began to speak.

"The good it does depends on many things, my daughter. It depends most of all on the faith of the one who made the *paho*. If all those things I mentioned are inside the little bundle that it carries on its back, it would mean that the one making the *paho* planted it in Mother Earth as a prayer for a plentiful harvest, with moisture enough to help Earth produce full ears of corn, plump beans, sweet melons." He looked up at her and his small face was worried. "Surely you have not forgotten the meaning of the feather? Feathers represent the spirits that are in all things. This one represents the spirit that is in the prayer the *paho* offers up."

Polingaysi turned away and took the *paho* in her hands. About to tear open the cornhusk, she looked down to see her father's hands stilled and horror in his expression. Suddenly she could not open the *paho's* treasure without his permission. She could not fly in the face of tradition to that extent, knowing it would offend his spirit, however silent he remained, however little he reproached her openly.

"May I open it?"

Her father bent his head, possibly questioning the propriety of such an action and fearing the harm it might do him and his daughter. After a moment of hesitation, he sighed, saying, "It seems well weathered. I think it is more than four days old. If so, its purpose has been served and the power has left it. Use your left hand."

Gently, in spite of her pretended scorn, Polingaysi opened the bit of wrapped cornhusk. It had been folded while still green into a tiny triangle. In this little pouch there was a bit of material about the size of a pea. Seeds, cornmeal, pollen, held together with honey, as her father had predicted.

"Can't you see there's nothing of value in here?" Polingaysi cried.

"Not to you," her father agreed. "Not to me. But to the one who made it in prayer."

She would have questioned him further, but he took his work and went outside, his face enigmatic.

"For pity's sake, Mother," Polingaysi burst out, turning to Sevenka who had been working quietly on a basket during the discussion, "does everything in the life of a Hopi have a hidden meaning? Why, for instance, should I use my left hand to open that thing?"

"It seems foolish to you because you are young and do not understand everything," her mother said patiently. "Perhaps you are foolish because you do not understand Hopi ways, though you are a Hopi. I will tell you about the left hand.

"The left hand is on the heart side of the body. It is the hand that moves most slowly. It selects, instead of grabbing as the right hand does. It is cleaner. It does not touch the mouth during the eating of food, nor does it clean the body after release of waste materials.

"Do you remember watching our medicine man—the Man With Eyes—at his work? In his healing rites and also in his religious ceremonies he uses the left hand, for those reasons I have just given you. The left hand, then, is the hand that is of the heart and the spirit, not of nature and the earth."

Polingaysi struggled to deny the beauty of the words her mother had spoken. She sought a scoffing answer, but found none. After a moment the older woman continued.

"One more thing I will tell you about the *pahos*. They must be kept free of the white man's ways if they are to have the full power of old times. That is why Hopi people do not sharpen them to a point with white man's steel blades, but grind them to sharpness on sandstone."

At that moment Polingaysi saw one of her mother's brothers passing the window. He knew nothing of the discussion and she had no desire to reopen it. With her left hand she placed the *paho* on the window sill.

"Polingaysi!" the old man cried, his face crinkling into a big smile of welcome. "It is a great treat to my spirit to see you after so long a time. We are always happy to see our child come home, even if she does make us sit at a wooden platform when we eat."

Polingaysi lost some of her contentiousness and laughed. He had always complained about sitting at the table, insisting that he could not keep his feet warm while he was eating unless he sat on them, Hopi-fashion. Her little grandmother had been completely mystified by the table, and though Polingaysi had patiently explained its use, the old lady had laboriously climbed up onto it, instead of seating herself on the wooden bench that served as a chair.

She looked at her uncle and thought of all the new ideas she had gleaned during her life among white people. The old man had no desire to share her knowledge. To him the old way was best. He asked little of life: enough food to keep the breath in his thin, worn old body, a little heat in the fireplace, a drink of water when he was dry.

It was she who was forever holding out her cup to be filled with knowledge.

SEVEN

IN THE TRADITIONAL Hopi pattern, children are advised, instructed, scolded, and sometimes punished, by their maternal uncles. Polingaysi's relations with her mother's brothers had been pleasant, but after she became a member of the Frey household, her old uncle in Moenkopi village began showing disapproval of her. Cousins repeated small remarks he had made about her and she became increasingly aware of his annoyance.

One day he sent word for her to come visit him. She went, to find him in a state of indignation. He began scolding at once.

"You proud and stubborn girl! Why are you straying from the Hopi way of life? Don't you know it is not good for a Hopi to be proud? Haven't I told you a Hopi must not pretend to hold himself above his people? Why do you keep trying to be a white man? You are a Hopi. Go home. Marry in the Hopi way. Have children." His eyes were angry and his mouth contemptuous. "I have said you were Hopi, but you are no longer a true Hopi. You don't know the Hopi way. In a year or so, even if you do go back to Oraibi, you won't know anything. Leave these white people who are leading you away from your own beliefs. Go. Go now."

Tears streamed down Polingaysi's cheeks as she listened to the man's bitter words. All her inner confusion, all her painful indecision, swelled in her breast until she could bear it no longer. She lashed back at him.

"I won't! I won't go back to the life of a pagan. Never, never again. I've worked for this education you ridicule. At Riverside, I scrubbed miles of dirty floors while I was learning a little about reading and writing and arithmetic. After I learned to sew, I made dresses for others, bending over the sewing machine while the other girls slept, to earn money for my own dresses.

"I've worked hard for everything I have. It has not been easy for me to learn this new way of living. Do you think I'll go back to sleeping on the floor and eating out of a single pot? Do you think I want to have a household of children who are always hungry and in rags, as I was in my childhood? No! I don't care what you think of me. I don't care what my Hopi people think. Not any more. I'm going to keep on learning, no matter how much you despise me for it."

Trembling violently, she turned on her heel and left his house, amazed at her temerity. How could she have dared talk in those defiant terms to an uncle? It frightened her. She could see the chasm between her two worlds widening; his words had stung like the lashes of the Whipper Kachina on the day of her initiation into the Kachina cult.

She had expected those initiatory lashes. Only Hopi children initiated into the Powamua fraternity escape them. She had looked forward to them as an opening of the door to wisdom.

As she walked swiftly toward the Frey home on the hillside, smarting under the injustice of her uncle's reproaches, she recalled the day of her initiation.

Feeling important and excited, she had walked between her ceremonial "parents" to the kiva, her shoulder blanket clutched close to shield her body from the February chill. The arms of the ladder had seemed to reach out to her, and she had gone into them and down the rungs into the dim warmth of the kiva.

Other initiates sat on the plastered stone bench between their sponsors, feet drawn up, simulating young eagles in the nest. Before she joined them she saw the feathers dangling from a peg on the wall, and the beautiful little sand mosaic beneath them. It was only after she was seated that she saw the larger sandpainting on which she would later stand for whipping.

She began to be afraid. The other children also were fearful. Then an old man, naked except for a G-string, came down the ladder and began addressing the initiates. He spoke rapidly and in low tones. Although she listened intently, Polingaysi could not hear all of his words, but she realized that he was telling the ancient history of the Hopis and of their migrations from the beginning.

There was an air of expectancy on the part of the older people as the old man left the kiva, and suddenly there was a fearful din at the kiva opening, a sound of running feet, a beating of yucca lashes against the standard.

Hearts racing, the candidates for initiation stared at the kiva opening. Two Hu Kachinas, their bodies painted black with white spots, rushed down the ladder carrying armfuls of yucca lashes. They wore nothing except red moccasins, breech clout, mask, and foxskin ruff. The masks were black and bulging-eyed, with horns at each side, white spots on the cheeks, and a white turkey track in the center of each forehead.

Crow Mother, Ang-wu-sna-som-ta-qa, which is to say "Man With Crow Wings Tied To," followed, wearing a woman's dress and ceremonial robe with moccasins, and carrying additional pale green yucca lashes for the whippers. Her mask had great black crow wings at each side.

At once a little boy was led forward by his sponsors, his naked body trembling. Stepping into the large sandpainting, he raised one hand above his head and covered his genitals with the other. The lashes curled about his body, leaving welts, then his godfather pulled him aside and took the remainder of the whipping for him.

When her turn came, Polingaysi was grateful that she was a girl and was allowed to wear her blanket dress. The whipping she received was not painful, but the emotional strain sent her to the bench weeping and weak. It seemed cruel to her that Crow Mother should urge the whippers to strike harder. However, when the whippers whipped each other at the conclusion of the rites, she felt better. Justice had been done.

The Powamua chief then dismissed the Kachinas with gifts of breath feathers and cornmeal and began his lecture. The initiates were now at the threshold of knowledge, he told them. They would learn more secrets soon, but must not tell the younger, uninitiated children what had taken place. Telling, they were warned, would bring reprisals from the angry Kachinas.

Reaching the Freys' houseyard, Polingaysi looked down into the narrow streets of the old village of Moenkopi, the rock houses huddled on the lower slopes of the sand-dune-bordered wash.

"That initiation!" she thought angrily. "What was it but a pagan rite? I must forget it."

Not yet calm enough to talk with the Freys about her clash with the old uncle, she went to her room. Turning toward the mirror, she surveyed her solemn reflection unapprovingly.

"Maybe I'm not a true Hopi. But what am I? Am I a true anything? Am I sincere? Do I really want to waste my time in trying to bring the gospel to my stubborn, superstition-bound Hopi people? They will only despise me for it."

She began taking the pins from her long and heavy black hair, intending to wash it. Suddenly she realized how automatic the gesture had been, how Hopi. Wash the hair. Purify the life stream.

In ancient days, her mother had told her, it had been considered a sin to cut the hair, except as ritual decreed. When the white men came, they insisted that the Hopi men have their long hair cut. When they refused, the white men cut their hair by force, disgracing them in the eyes of their people.

Hesitating, Polingaysi brushed her hair thoughtfully. There was no denying that the Hopi way was rich in symbolism. It was no wonder that cutting the "stream of life" had seemed sacrilegious to them, steeped as they were in the belief that anything that had to do with moisture was to be held in reverence.

Combings and cuttings of hair were saved and made into a hair cord to be used ceremonially. The bridegroom's father, for instance, provided cord from the family savings for the new hairdress of his son's bride. The paternal grandmother used hair from the family hoard when it was time for her to dress a granddaughter's hair in the tight little buds of the *be-lon-so-mi,* the "maiden" buds of a girl just coming into womanhood. Babies had their first haircut at the time of the February Batsavu ceremony associated with the Bean Dance. A strange haircut it was, too, leaving the child looking only half shorn.

There were many symbolic references to hair in the Hopi pattern life. Likened to hair were Mother Corn's silken strands that fell over the developing ear with its plump kernels. A Hopi farmer would instinctively protect this silken fall, knowing it would wither and fall away when the life cycle of the ear's growth had been completed.

Polingaysi admitted the beauty of the *poliene,* or butterfly wing, coiffure of mature maidens, though she thought it foolish to take time to have the hair wound on the U-shaped sticks.

At that time, most of the older women, conservative Sevenka among them, wore their hair in thick twisted rolls that hung forward over their shoulders, and many of them still clung to the traditional, handwoven, dark-blue blanket dress that fastened on the right shoulder, leaving the left shoulder bare.

She could remember when the men wore their hair long and loose-flowing, or caught up into a yarn-wrapped bun at the nape of the neck. Now, many of them cropped their hair and wore a bright band around their bangs.

Times were changing, changing even the tradition-bound Hopi.

Calmed by her reflections, she joined the Frey family and told the Reverend Frey and Mrs. Frey of her clash with the uncle. They understood her anguish of mind. As a Hopi, she was misunderstood by the white man; as a convert of the missionaries, she was looked upon with suspicion by the Hopi people. Her restlessness, her moments of depression, were the inevitable result of her desire to be different, to make a new place for herself in a world that sometimes seemed determined not to allow her a place in it.

As usual, the Freys did all in their power to help her. The Reverend Frey was about to make a trip to Newton, Kansas. He published a small church paper, which he ran off on a hand press, and he had it in mind to print translations of Bible verses and stories in the Hopi language. In Newton there was a small printing office where Polingaysi might learn the type cases, so that she could assist him when they returned to Moenkopi.

Polingaysi was all eagerness to begin the eastward journey. She had seen a little of the far West; this would be something entirely new.

EIGHT

SHE WAS NOT disappointed. As the train rolled through the rich farm lands of Kansas, Polingaysi thought of the Pacific Ocean, stretching out into misty distance. She thought of the desert, its colored bands narrowing and softening in tone in the distance. Here the golden fields swept off and away to the top of the hills and beyond.

It was the harvest season. There was a hustle and bustle of preparation for the coming winter. Corn stood in tall shocks, golden pumpkins at their base. Onions and potatoes were being sacked.

So much food. So much food everywhere—except in Hopiland. It seemed unfair that these people should have so much when the Hopi farmer had so little.

As they neared their destination Polingaysi began to worry about her appearance. The Freys had received a box of shoes and clothing and from this miscellany her outfit had been chosen. The shoes did not fit her feet. The dress, though of good material, was not suitable for a young girl.

She need not have worried. The Reverend Frey's younger brother, John, came to meet them and to take them to his farm about fifteen miles from town. His wife and his mother came hurrying from the house to greet them, and neither of them was better dressed than Polingaysi, though no doubt their shoes fit their feet better. The older woman wore a dark dress, the skirt barely clearing the ground; young Mrs. Frey's dark cotton was also simply made and very long. They spoke only German, but their warmth and friendliness spoke in tones the Hopi girl could not help understanding. She liked them both and felt secure and at ease with them, a wanted guest.

Dinner was waiting on the big table. Again Polingaysi was impressed by the quantities of food. While they spoke to each other in a language she did not understand, she ate heartily. The Reverend Frey was considerate. When the conversation turned to subjects in which she might be interested he kindly included her, drawing her out and interpreting her comments for his relatives.

The telephone began ringing before they had finished their noonday repast. The Reverend Frey was asked to speak at several Mennonite churches in the area. He and Polingaysi were invited to dine and visit at homes of his many relatives. Polingaysi, pleased to see how greatly loved was her good friend, looked forward to the stay with heightened interest.

The next morning she went with the missionary to a small shop where she was to receive instruction in typesetting. At first it embarrassed her to sit on the high stool in front of the type case, but she forgot herself as she became interested in the placement of the type and the method of transferring it from case to composer's stick. By night she had decided it was not going to be difficult for her to learn this work, but that it was far from being the sort of employment she wanted.

She paid no attention to the young men who worked in the shop. Keenly aware of her dark skin and Indian background, she was chary of courting slights or ill-mannered remarks. She was quiet and reserved, self-effacing as a frightened mouse.

It was different in the churches. She felt that the Mennonite people were her friends, that they were predisposed toward her not only because of the Reverend Frey but because they liked to hear her sing the old hymns they all knew so well. She sang earnestly and humbly, grateful for this one blessed talent.

It was with pleasure that she accompanied the Reverend Frey on a visit to the H. R. Voth home in Newton. Voth was the old friend of her family for whom her father had worked for so many years, and it was Voth who had taken Qoyawayma with him to this same Mennonite community, dressed him in white man's clothing, and shown him the wonders of civilization. Voth was eager for her to visit Bethel Academy and meet some of the faculty.

"When I took your father to the Academy," he told Polingaysi, "he looked the place over and said he hoped some one of his children would be able to go to school here. Perhaps you will be the one."

A sudden desire to be that one was awakened in the girl's heart. She saw the school as her father must have seen it, a splendid place after the poverty of the mesas. It would be wonderful to attend school there.

Voth's idea of winning people to Christianity had seemed to be based on breaking down their former beliefs, on making them ashamed of them. At that time Polingaysi the fledgling missionary, was almost fully convinced this was indeed the only method, while her Hopi elders on the reservation were incensed that Voth, presumably their friend, was revealing one by one their ceremonial secrets to magazines and museums.

"I remember when my father returned from here," she told Voth. "He brought each of us a present. Mine was a piece of red cotton material which I wore like a shawl over my blanket dress."

One Sunday morning during the church service, Polingaysi became aware of the shy regard of a blue-eyed German girl in the congregation. Again and again, she saw the girl look toward her and away. She became annoyed. Hopi-like, she thought it was not polite for the girl to keep looking at her. What was wrong with her, that she drew the girl's attention? She was flustered when, after service, she saw the girl coming toward her.

"I am Elizabeth Schmidt," the girl introduced herself timidly. "I have heard you, too, are named Elizabeth. I am hoping we can become friends."

Polingaysi was cool toward her, and suspicious. No one had ever before come to her impulsively offering friendship. What did the girl want of her? Later, Elizabeth Schmidt told the Indian girl how hurt she had been by the coolness. She had gone home weeping to tell her parents of the encounter.

"That poor little Indian girl. Those sad black eyes. She looks so lost and frightened and lonely." Those were her words and her parents were sympathetic. They invited the Reverend Frey to bring Polingaysi to their home. There she met the other Schmidt children—Mary, Philip, Isaac, and Frank. The younger Schmidts spoke good English, and the parents also tried for Polingaysi's sake to speak in the language she understood. They loved music and at Isaac's insistence she sang for them, "Star of the East."

Gradually Polingaysi let down her guard and had a wonderful time with the Schmidt's. She never ceased to be overwhelmed by the stores of food in the cellar, the great crocks of butter, the barrels of pickles, the rows of jars on the shelves: peaches, pears, tomatoes, cherries, relishes, sweet corn. Often she thought, "If my mother could see all this food! If she could just see it!" It would be difficult to make her believe that one family could have so much stored away.

In little bursts of confidence Polingaysi told them stories of her people, about their struggle to grow crops in the arid desert lands and their never-ending prayers for rain. Schmidt and his sons shook their heads in amazement when she demonstrated the Hopi method of planting corn at the foot of a sand dune, boring into the soil with a planting stick. The entire family listened in rapt silence when she told of the life of the village.

She told them how the villagers sought the *piki* stone, planning the excursion far in advance and proceeding according to set ritual, treating the stone as a sacred maiden who was to serve the family in whose home it would be installed. And how, after it had been ground down and smoothed and oiled with chewed watermelon seed, and finally carefully tempered, the woman who made *piki* on it for the first time fed the first tissue-thin sheet of *piki* to the flames as a gift to the "maiden."

She told them about bartering in the village as she had known it in her youth. There was a place where those who wished to trade wares usually sat. Bartering days were anticipated with relish, since they not only provided redistribution of food and household goods, but gave the older women a chance to "mend the garments of their ancestors," as they said, telling the old tales over and nodding their heads with pleasure in remembering.

The village crier always announced the impending activity from a housetop, and the women came, bringing whatever they had to barter. Corn, of course. Sweet corn, and field corn of many colors. Cornmeal, solidly packed on a plaque and covered with a cloth. Pumpkin seeds, beans, dried squash, desert greens if the season was right for them, jerky, perhaps a freshly killed rabbit or so, even desert grass seed to be used in *pikami*.

She told them how the women would cry out, "These good Hopi beans want dried peaches." Or, "These greens are crying for fresh rabbit meat." And how occasionally the aunts of some bartering woman would tease her, the maternal aunts scolding because she elected to trade for cornmeal instead of grinding it, and the paternal aunts defending her by telling how early she got up in the morning to pick the greens she offered in return for meal.

Her thoughts were on the mesas as she told them of hearing the men leaving for the fields at dawn of a summer morning and their echoing cries of *"Bow-hai, bow-hai-hi."* And sometimes when she finished talking about the ways of home, she was lonely, with the strange loneliness of one who feels he has lost something but isn't quite sure what it is that is missing.

Sometimes she apologized for the ignorance of her people, but more often she defended them. "They have believed as they do for many centuries. It is not easy to lead them upon a new trail."

With people like the Schmidts, the Voths, and the Freys, Polingaysi could relax, but there were others in that Kansas community who made her keenly aware of the fact that she was not a white girl. A startled glance, a sharp withdrawal of person, made her suffer as though blows had been rained upon her.

One day she went with the Reverend Frey to a small restaurant and was refused service. The missionary gently rebuked the gum-chewing waitress but she said stubbornly, "We don't serve colored." Even when he called the manager and told him Polingaysi was a true American native, an American Indian, the waitress glared at Polingaysi.

"Please, please," Polingaysi begged, getting up and going to the door, tears rolling down her cheeks, "I don't want to eat here. I couldn't swallow the food."

The incident made a deep wound which had not healed before a child probed it unwittingly. "That woman didn't wash her face and hands," he piped up before his mother could hush him.

Often, thinking about these incidents brought tears to Polingaysi's eyes. What can one do about one's skin? We, who are clay blended by the Master Potter, come from the kiln of Creation in many hues. How can people say one skin is colored, when each has its own coloration? What should it matter that one bowl is dark and the other pale, if each is of good design and serves its purpose well?

The time of their stay passed quickly, and almost before she knew it, Polingaysi was packing for the return trip. Now her suitcase had in it some new, up-to-date dresses. Elizabeth Schmidt, who loved to sew, had made Polingaysi dresses like her own, the same material and design, though much smaller, Polingaysi being less than five feet tall and weighing barely ninety pounds.

On the return train trip to Arizona, Polingaysi confided to the Reverend Frey her new ambition to study at the Academy if it could be arranged. She had learned to set type and would do it gladly, but it was routine work with no challenge for her. Her big challenge was in education.

The missionary considered the problem with characteristic realism. How would she pay her way through the Academy. If that problem could be solved satisfactorily, the training would be valuable to her. In three years she would be a trained worker in the mission field. She would have a definite purpose in life.

"There is the kitchen," Polingaysi reminded him. "I can wash dishes. I can wait on tables. I can even cook a little. I'm sure I can do enough work to pay my tuition."

The Reverend Frey was in accord. He promised to help her work out the details and make preparations for a three-year course at the Academy.

Meanwhile, they returned to Moenkopi and the work at hand, but as she set type or helped Mrs. Frey in the house, Polingaysi dreamed of the future. She reminded her father of his conversation with Voth during his own short visit to Newton and he nodded, recalling his words in regard to the Academy.

"I will be the one of your children to attend that school," Polingaysi declared. "Next year, I shall go there."

His eyes were bright with interest. Yes, he told her, that would be a good thing. The people there were kind. They would help her.

She returned to Kansas the next summer to stay at the Frey farm and work for Mrs. John Frey. Until then she had had only a vague idea of the hard life of a farm woman.

Breakfast was at sunrise. Then there was dinner, mid-afternoon lunch, and late supper. The day was a long one of preparing and serving food and clearing up the dishes, pots, and pans.

The women worked as hard as did the sturdy men, she discovered. They raised chickens, pigs, and gardens, helped with the milking, and took care of the milk and cream. They sewed and washed and ironed, took care of the babies, and still found time for church work.

Polingaysi thought of the Hopi women, slaving at their grinding stones, and the German women slaving over their washboards, and wondered which were to be more pitied. At least, the German women had plenty of water, with windmills furnishing the pumping power, their bright blades turning as the prairie wind blew. The Hopi women still carried water, from the spring at Old Oraibi and from the village spring at New Oraibi.

The Freys had a stove made of firebrick in their wash house. It had two big fire boxes and a huge oven. Two shining wash boilers were set on top for the heating of wash water and the boiling of the white pieces. While the women scrubbed and boiled and rinsed and hung the washing, long loaves of fragrant bread baked, filling the air with mouth-watering fragrance, and at the same time taking advantage of the heated stove.

After a week of dawn-to-dark labor, Polingaysi was eager for Sunday, day of rest. Everyone of that household went to church, dressed with quiet neatness in immaculately clean clothing. Sometimes, as they listened solemnly to solemn services, Polingaysi, who loved to laugh, moved restlessly in her seat, wondering if the minister ever smiled. His was a mournful, depressing approach to religion, and the Indian girl was not to be blamed if now and then, by way of contrast, she thought of the flash and color and rhythm of Kachina dancing in sun-flooded plazas at home.

The summer waned and school began. Polingaysi enrolled at Bethel Academy as Elizabeth Ruth Qoyawayma. As she had prophesied in her first conversation with the Reverend Frey about her attendance at the Academy, the management found a place for her on the kitchen and dining-room staff. She would be waitress and dishwasher, and in this way pay her tuition.

She was a cheerful worker, but the hours were long and there were times when she felt that she would drop from fatigue. She kept her trials to herself. She had asked for this experience; she would bear her burden without complaints.

To her great delight, she was able to continue the musical education begun at Riverside and encouraged by the Freys. She received vocal instruction, as well as lessons in piano. Her singing brought her much praise, soothing her sometimes troubled and uncertain thoughts. It was good, oh, so good, to have a talent recognized and enjoyed by others. It was a means of communication, beyond language, leaping all barriers.

Her friendship with Elizabeth Schmidt continued, grew, and became so firmly established that it would last a lifetime. They were so often together that they were called the "two Elizabeths." No two girls could have been less alike in outward appearance nor more closely attuned in spirit.

Elizabeth Schmidt's birthday was April 9 and her parents were giving a party for her. They invited Polingaysi. She accepted, saying she wished she had a birthday to celebrate. They thought it a joke at first, then were shocked to discover that she did not know her birthdate, except that it was sometime in the spring of the year.

What were dates to the old-time Hopi? What did days and months mean to them? They lived the days as they came and were not concerned with the length of their sojourn on earth. While they lived, there was work to be done. When they grew small in old age they would travel on into the afterworld of the spirit.

Generously, Elizabeth Schmidt offered to share her birthday with Polingaysi, and her birthday party as well. And so it was.

Polingaysi proudly shared her friend's birthday and was not after that concerned about the actual date of her own birth.

The months rolled past so rapidly that summer vacation arrived fast on the heels of April, when she had celebrated her supposed nineteenth birthday. She returned to Arizona, almost hysterically eager to see her parents and her brothers and sisters. But when she reached Oraibi she was shocked to see how unkempt they were. Was it possible they had always looked like this and she was only now aware of it? She would have to do something about this. Immediately.

Unaware of her disapproval, her parents greeted her with warmth. Their smiles enfolded her in love. Oh, how dearly she loved them. But they were still unconverted to Christianity. She must bring them into her new world of enlightenment as soon as possible.

They listened to her politely, but without response. For the time being, her efforts to lead them into her own religious thought were rejected. What could she do, she asked herself, to prove that she wanted to help them, and that the white man's way was the one right way?

White man! She had heard those words spoken so many times with indignation, hatred, resentment, ridicule, but never with love, by the Hopi. To be sure, they loved the gentle Freys, but they made no exceptions generally, and Polingaysi, for all her white contacts, was at times as contemptuous and suspicious as the most conservative Hopi. Her change of heart, which should have been brought about by the love showered upon her by the Schmidts and the Freys, came slowly.

The past kept bobbing up in her mind. She remembered the white men, flanked by Navajo police, who snatched children from parents and herded them off to the government schools. She remembered the shocking punishment of the children by government teachers. She had seen grown Hopi men crying because white men had cut their hair. Worst of all, she had seen women stripped and marched through a dipping vat like so many cattle, because—so the white man claimed—an epidemic threatened the reservation residents. This was a thing no Hopi woman could forgive. Children may run naked, but grown girls and women are modest. To force the exposure of their bodies in this way had been unthinkable.

She wavered, secretly, and was unhappy because of it. It was a relief to return to Kansas.

The second summer Polingaysi and another Hopi girl went with the Reverend Frey to Beatrice, Nebraska, to visit missionary groups of the Mennonite church. It was a surprise to them to see women of all ages busily working on baby clothes, quilts, aprons, dresses, and other articles for distribution to needy Indian homes. Many boxes were already packed for shipping and the girls were enthusiastically received by the workers.

Since the German people of that community spoke good English, it was possible for Polingaysi and her friend to talk to them, even to the older people. They thought it odd that the Mennonites of that area were so similarly dressed as almost to appear to be in uniform.

This visit led to another in Oklahoma a short time later. The mission where they were to be guests for a few days was on an Indian reservation. Those Indians were tall and big-boned and many of them were fat. The little Hopi girls felt even smaller in comparison, but again communication was possible since all the younger Indians spoke English.

In the gathering at the mission chapel there was a very old man who spoke no English. Introduced to the guests, he stared intently at them, then made a remark which the missionary interpreted.

"He says he has been to your country where the people live in rock houses on top of the rocks. He says he went there with a raiding party many moons ago when he was young."

Of especial interest to the Hopi girls, accustomed as they were to ceremonial dancing, was the place near the mission where this tribe of Indians had just finished their four-day Sun Dance ritual. There had been, they were told, a circular shelter of poles with a tall cottonwood log in the center to which thongs had been attached. A man wishing to show his bravery and devotion tied the other end of a thong to himself, by making a slit in his flesh. Then he danced until the flesh gave way, freeing him. One dancer, the missionary told them, had been carried away supposedly dead. When the dancer regained consciousness and returned to his own home, his people were afraid of him and drove him away.

Discussing these customs later, Polingaysi and her friend expressed their amazement. Those who called the Kachina dances pagan should attend a Sun Dance, they agreed.

It was as dusty and hot on this reservation as it was in Hopiland. The girls were glad to return to Newton, while the Reverend Frey continued his mission tour.

Polingaysi thought ahead to the end of her training at the Academy with growing apprehension. Brave in some ways, she was a coward in others. She dreaded the active work in the religious field that she would be expected to do among her own people.

NINE

WHEN SHE RETURNED to Hopiland in the early summer of 1914, Polingaysi had a frightening sense of being enfolded in the old ways. It was as though the mesas reached out to claim her, gently but firmly, and press her once more into the culture pattern.

She had struggled to get away; she had accepted a challenge, and was determined to profit by her years at the Academy. She buried herself in work at the Frey mission in Moenkopi and at the Mennonite mission near Oraibi.

The first mission, occupied by the Reverend Voth and his family, had been built about two miles below Old Oraibi and across the Oraibi Wash on land given to Voth by Chief Lololoma. Polingaysi's father had helped to construct those buildings. As it later proved, they were too close to the edge of the ever-deepening gulch. The water swirled the loose sand downstream and undermined the mission property.

Another spot of land nearer Oraibi was assigned to the Mennonites and a new mission was constructed. Polingaysi was to work from this mission, making home visitations and interpreting for field workers. One of these was a friendly young woman whose name was Caroline Burkholder. Polingaysi soon became much attached to her and was happy in the association.

One windy morning they rented horses from Charles, brother

of Chief Tawaquaptewa and brother-in-law of Polingaysi, with the intention of interviewing several families at distant points of the reservation. A storm threatened and Polingaysi, disregarding the skittishness of her mount, tied her raincoat behind her saddle. The girls set off at a trot but had gone only a short distance when the wind flapped Polingaysi's raincoat, causing her horse to buck. She knew nothing about riding. She grabbed the saddle-horn, but it was not enough. Another jump or so and her grip loosened. As she fell, she caught a glimpse of lashing hind legs and rolled away from that danger.

Getting up quickly, she felt herself cautiously, encouraged to find no bones broken. However, after a few days of soreness, she discovered that lifting or other hard work was painful. She shunned horseback riding from then on. Eventually she learned that she had been injured internally by the fall and surgery was required to mend the damage.

Her work on the reservation did not bring her satisfaction. Her Hopi friends listened politely but were not converted from their pattern of life. She was ready for a change when the Reverend Frey asked her and another Hopi girl to go with him to a Mennonite general conference in Pennsylvania. Polingaysi accepted at once, eager as she was to see more of the United States.

The Reverend Frey was able to secure passes on the Santa Fe Railroad, and he scheduled a tour of considerable length, with appearances at many churches and missions throughout the East.

Polingaysi and her friend Minnie were excited to be riding in a Pullman, but a trifle ill at ease when white people turned upon them questioning and disapproving glances. Now and then someone asked them point-blank about their racial strain. They were glad to reach the Mennonite communities, where dark skin raised no questions and brought no indignant stares.

Their first engagement was at a church a few miles from

Philadelphia. As usual the Reverend Frey told of his work among the Hopi Indians, and Polingaysi sang. Minnie's part in the venture was to give a testimony of her conversion to Christianity.

Polingaysi forgot many of the churches and congregations they visited, but she always remembered that history began to mean something to her during this tour. The Reverend Frey pointed out Philadelphia's historic buildings. She thought she had never seen anything more beautiful than Mount Vernon, or more fascinating than the work of glass blowers at the glass factory in Altoona, Pennsylvania.

In Washington they saw the Capitol building and the White House, visited the Indian Bureau and were shown through the building by one of the employees.

On their way back to Arizona, they spent a little time in Indiana, where Polingaysi was impressed by the hills and valleys, the thick stands of trees, and the beautiful winding roads of the countryside. Again among the Mennonites, they went through the regular routine of church and social gatherings, then went on to Kansas to renew acquaintance with old friends before returning to Hopiland.

About two miles from Moenkopi, at Tuba City, was an Indian boarding school, attended mostly by Navajo children. A temporary employee there was Rena Edwardson, a calm, quiet, kind young woman from the East, who had come west to visit relatives and remained because she loved the western scene. She had taught Navajo beginners, ranging from tots of five to teenagers, for a three-week period, pending the arrival of the Indian Service teacher of that room. In the fall of 1918 she was asked to take a position as matron of the Kayenta Indian boarding school, about seventy-five miles north of Tuba City, near the Utah state line.

Polingaysi had met Rena and liked her. Therefore, when she was asked to go to Kayenta as Rena's assistant, she welcomed the opportunity. Unsure as she was of her ability to convert her own people, she was glad to have a respite from missionary work.

A Kayenta stockman came for them, driving two white mules hitched to a covered wagon. He was a true Westerner, from cowboy boots to easy, drawling speech and big hat. Early in the morning they started on the three-day journey across the lonely Navajo reservation. In the wagon box were the girls' trunks and boxes, three barrels of water, feed for the mules, and a stock of provisions for the boarding school.

Rena, a splendid cook, had seen to it that they had camping necessities and food for the long trip, including roast beef, ham, bacon, fried chicken, eggs, potatoes, coffee, and bread.

The September weather was perfect—the air clear and cool, the sun warm. The driver kept them amused with stories, and occasionally Polingaysi sang. Almost before they knew it the sun was low in the west. They had planned to spend the night at Red Lake Trading Post, but when they pulled up in the front yard the trader came to the door to tell them his wife was ill with influenza and the doctor had warned him not to allow anyone to come into the store or the house, lest the disease spread.

There was nothing to do but sleep outside on the ground. During the night a brisk shower awakened the girls, but they pulled the tarpaulin over their heads and went back to sleep. They were on their way before sunrise.

When they tired of jouncing along in the wagon, the girls got out and walked. The second night they camped in a little forest of pinyon trees, built a campfire and prepared their evening meal, then again made their beds on the ground. The night was clear and still and moonlit. Now and then there was the clink of hobbles as the white mules grazed nearby.

Polingaysi slipped out of bed early and climbed the nearest hill. Some of the trees were loaded with pinyon nuts, so she gathered them, unaware of the passing of time. She returned to find biscuits baking in the dutch oven, bacon frying over the campfire, and coffee boiling in a big granite coffeepot. Rena was nowhere in sight.

"She went looking for you," the driver drawled, turning the bacon, "thought you'd get lost. I told her she didn't need to worry about an Indian losing her directions." Polingaysi called and her new friend returned, relief plain on her face.

As they drove slowly through Marsh Pass that third day, the driver told them stories of the great Indian ruins to the north, Betatakin and Keet Seel. They could see for miles in all directions, but in all that distance there were no buildings except an occasional Navajo hogan, mud covered and distinguishable only if there was smoke coming from its smokehole. Now and then a rider moved along the horizon, or they heard the tinkle of bells and saw a band of sheep being driven by a Navajo woman or child.

The road was terrifyingly narrow in spots and very rough. Rains had caused washouts and portions of the cliffs along which the road wound had fallen, but the driver seemed unconcerned. When the black shaft of Agathla Peak showed in the distance, he told them they were " 'bout there now," and slapped the tired mules into a brisker pace.

It was sundown when they reached the little settlement of Kayenta, consisting of Wetherill's, Colville's, and Babbitt's trading posts, and boasting a population of about fifteen white people. It was a trading center for the thousands of Navajo Indians who shifted back and forth over the reservation, seeking grazing for their sheep, goats, and horses.

The boarding school was a lonely and bare place with a dormitory that looked large and ghostly in the dim light of a kerosene lantern with a smoked chimney. In spite of the welcome they received from the principal and his wife, who had been there a month getting the school ready, Polingaysi broke down and cried, while Rena, in her serene way, tried to cheer her.

The outlook was less grim in the sunshine of the next morning. The girls went for a walk before breakfast and enjoyed the magnificent scenery—the Black Mountains to one side, the spires and buttes of Monument Valley to the other.

They visited with the principal and his wife and were briefed on their duties. The principal, they soon realized, was more interested in the book he was writing about the Indian ruins nearby than in the operation of the school.

Lunch over, they were unpacking leisurely when a small car rattled up and an excited man jumped out to deliver a note from the superintendent of schools at Tuba City. The note informed the Kayenta principal that a wave of influenza had struck Tuba City. All but three of the children and most of the employees were sick in bed.

The girls replaced the clothing they had just unpacked, the principal and his wife packed hastily, and all four got into the car for the jolting trip back to Tuba City.

They found the hospital overflowing with patients. Teachers, cooks, nurses, parents, children—all had been stricken almost overnight. Flagstaff, the nearest town, could not send help, since it was hard hit and also needed assistance to care for the sick.

Polingaysi did all she could to assist in the emergency, but she soon succumbed to the disease and took her turn in the hospital. When she was well enough, she returned to Moenkopi and the Frey home.

This was a time of sorrow on the Hopi reservation, where hundreds in the mesa villages lay in the rock houses, ill unto death. The Reverend Frey had a little knowledge of medicine; he was a devoted nurse, and he brought the gospel, as well as his willing hands, to aid the frightened afflicted Hopis who were in various stages of the disease. Those he could help, he helped to the limit of his ability; those who were at death's door were given comfort; those who died were prepared by him for burial, patiently and sorrowfully.

One day in November, the eleventh, the missionary came home with a glow of gladness in his face.

"The war is over," he told his family. "The armistice has been signed."

Polingaysi stared at him. The war had never seemed real to her; now it was over.

Teaching, except in Sunday school, had never entered Polingaysi's head, but because of the epidemic a chance to try was given her. She was asked to serve as a substitute in the Tuba City boarding school.

Caroline Burkholder, an ex-teacher herself, and Rena, who had distinguished herself by her heroic efforts in behalf of sick and dying influenza patients, encouraged Polingaysi to undertake the new occupation. But it was a nervous and apprehensive Polingaysi who entered the schoolroom that first morning and looked into the black eyes of some thirty Navajo pupils, ranging from six-year-olds to tall and gangling eighteen-year-old Pete.

Pete was literally her biggest problem. She suspected that Pete could speak a little English, but she couldn't get him to open his mouth, much less talk to her. He sat all day at his desk, watching her every move but ignoring her attempts to interest him in schoolwork. His lethargy made her fume with impatience. The Hopis and the Navajos were seldom sympathetic toward one another because of the past, and all the buried resentments began seething in Polingaysi.

That lazy Navajo. She knew well why he remained in school so placidly, eating three good meals a day, living in a warm, clean dormitory, and receiving good clothing. It was better than the hard, cold work of herding sheep in winter out on the reservation.

He could afford to endure the scolding of his little Hopi teacher, and to show his amusement at her bustling, bossy ways.

She was much more successful with the small children. At first they looked at her from their beautiful black eyes, fearful as little deer, but gradually she won their confidence.

From the first she saw the need of relating their schoolwork to their everyday experiences. She found a horned toad one day and brought it to the classroom with her, delighted to see their instant recognition and interest.

"That is my grandfather," one of the little boys said solemnly, but would not say more. Perhaps his family had a high regard for the little creatures, she decided, and went on with her teaching.

As her confidence grew, she felt she could no longer endure Pete's presence in her classroom. He did not belong there with the eager little ones. He was a bad influence. Besides, he irritated the teacher. One day she summoned him to her desk.

"Pete!" she said sharply, looking up into his intelligent handsome face. "If you're going to stay in school, you are going to have to do something. You can at least open your mouth and answer when I speak to you."

Pete grinned down at her, saying nothing, then returned to his seat and lounged there, uncommunicative as usual. After school she found a note on his desk. It was brief and to the point.

"Pete no good Navajo," the crudely printed words proclaimed. "No can learn."

He did not return to school and Polingaysi missed him. Her conscience nagged her. Judge not, lest ye also be judged, it reminded her. Perhaps she was at fault in not trying harder and with a more loving heart to help the lad. Perhaps he really wanted to learn, and had learned, judging from his printed note.

But Pete was gone, swallowed up in the vastness of the reservation. She never saw him again, but she remembered him more distinctly than any of the others.

Her first check brought with it the realization that teaching might be a means of building up her tiny nest egg to proportions that would allow her to begin construction of her own home. A monthly check gave her a rich feeling of independence. When the school term ended, she was more than willing to continue working at Tuba City as cook in the clubhouse where the government employees ate.

She decided to have a serious talk with the Freys about her future. Was she really qualified to be a missionary? Were they sure that was her field? Those were the questions she finally asked them. The sadness and disappointment in their kind faces stabbed her to the heart.

"They'll be glad to be rid of me, ungrateful Indian that I am," she thought, but this was not true.

They urged her, instead, not to lose what she had worked for so long. Probably, they said, she needed more religious knowledge and more training for missionary work. To correct this condition, they offered to enroll her in the Los Angeles Bible Institute for the fall session.

She was not strong enough to resist them, but she went to Los Angeles with a haunting doubt in her heart. She had learned well that any Hopi who, at that time, was not following the Hopi pattern was a misfit. She was no longer accepted as one of them. Her former Sherman schoolmates had returned, married, and were living the traditional life. She was still reaching out for education. What for? they would have asked. She would have answered with more heat than conviction. Sometimes she asked herself that very question: what for? Why, she thought, should she be so determined to learn, and learn, and learn?

The Reverend Frey went with her to Los Angeles. At the big building on Hill Street he talked with teachers and made arrangements for Polingaysi to do part-time work to help pay for her schooling. She was to sweep the second floor hallway in the morning and clean silverware in the school kitchen in the evening.

In order to continue with vocal training, she volunteered to take some of her money from the bank, though it was being hoarded for her dream house. But this was not necessary. The wife of one of the teachers gave her enough spare-time employment to take care of this need.

Her work at the teacher's home entailed some cooking. One day she was asked to prepare rice for dinner. Accustomed to cooking cornmeal, she had had no experience with rice, but it seemed simple enough. The rice was in a big jar. She wondered if there would be enough. She put five cupfuls in a pan and covered it with water, then set it on to cook. In a few minutes she had to add more water, then she had to find a larger kettle; and because she was used to stirring corn mush, she stirred the rice vigorously as it cooked. The result was a glutinous mess.

She told one of her classmates about her experience and the other girl laughed sympathetically, promising to teach her the proper way of cooking rice. The classmate was an eighteen-year-old Chinese girl from Shanghai, a Miss Yungu Zah, who had come to the United States knowing very little English, but with a great determination to learn.

She had an amazing memory. Once she heard a Bible verse she could repeat it perfectly. Often she and Polingaysi went up to the roof garden to repeat their verses to each other. When Polingaysi made a mistake, Yungu Zah would say, "Try again. You are not stupid." And Polingaysi would persist until she, too, could repeat the verse perfectly.

The cooking lesson was given in the Chinese girl's room, with the door closed and the blinds pulled, since it was against regulations to cook in one's room. Served with Chinese tea and pickled eggs brought from China, the rice was delicious.

Polingaysi was much pleased with her voice teacher, a small, round man with a splendid voice. He was a strict teacher and worked long and earnestly with Polingaysi to improve her pronunciation, especially of certain words. Honey, for instance. "Honey in the Rock" and "His Eye Is on the Sparrow," were two songs she sang well, as soon as she mastered the word "honey," which had a way of coming out "hohnee" at first.

She sang those songs many times in Los Angeles churches and was often soloist at the Church of the Open Door, where she was a member of the choir. Whenever her work had to do with music, she was happy.

She was also happy in the visitation work once a week, which was a feature of the course she was studying. Students went to county hospitals and old people's homes to visit the inmates and to help them in any way possible. Polingaysi enjoyed the old people especially. She thought of them as they had once been, useful and busy people with homes and children. Now, grouped together, they waited with patience for the end of their time.

She liked to sing for them and read the promises of the Bible, hoping that she was giving them the encouragement they needed to endure the waiting. When, one day, one little old lady called to another, "Oh, Mrs. Jones. Come on out. Our Indian girl is here," she was happy to be recognized and welcomed.

However, desert-born as she was, she never got used to the city. She had been sheltered in her own home, at the Sherman Institute, at the home of the Freys, and at Bethel Academy. She was frightened by the stories she had heard of white slavers and their activities in cities, and several experiences had intensified her fears.

One day she was returning from a visitation to the old people's home when a stranger sat down beside her and began to talk to her. She ignored him, but he persisted in annoying her, so she got off the car a block from her destination and drew a sigh of relief. Then she heard footsteps and, glancing back, she saw that the man was following her. He called to her, but she ran in terror, arriving breathless and weak to report the incident to the house matron and to be told that she did exactly right in running.

Another time she went on the train to Riverside to spend a Saturday with friends at Sherman Institute. One of the trainmen spoke to her, asking if she was an Indian and telling her he had lived in Arizona. He was in uniform, so the Hopi girl's fears were lulled and she talked to him. Then he asked her how she was going to get out to Sherman. She told him she always went out on the street car. He said the car didn't run any more, but that a friend of his would be in Riverside to meet him and he'd ask her to take Polingaysi on out.

Sure enough, there was a mannish-looking woman at the station and she, too, was in uniform.

"She'll take care of you," the man told Polingaysi as she got off the train. The woman came toward her, but again Polingaysi ran. The street car was coming. She got on and went her way with racing heart and a feeling of having escaped some dreadful fate.

When the Reverend Frey arrived, as usual with her welfare foremost in his mind, she had begun to wonder what she would do during the summer vacation. He knew of a lady who was to arrive about the time of the school's closing to spend the summer at Hermosa Beach, not far from Los Angeles. She and her retarded son would require the services of two women and a man, housekeeper, cook, and chauffeur. He thought Polingaysi might apply for work with this lady.

With a secret smile as she remembered her rice-cooking episode, Polingaysi said she would cook for them, if they liked her. She went with Frey to one of the large hotels for an interview and was all but overwhelmed by its grandeur. After a long wait, a stately lady all in black appeared, accompanied by a good-looking young man, who had nothing at all to say.

Polingaysi was employed. A few days later they picked her up at the Bible Institute and took her to the beach home where she was to spend the summer. It was not a large establishment. She and the housekeeper had to share a room. The chauffeur slept over the garage.

Polingaysi's heart went out to the son, a man in years, with wealth, health, and family background he could never appreciate. She was kind to him and he seemed to trust and like her. The big young man and the small Hopi woman often walked on the beach that summer, gathering sea shells and pretty pebbles.

Her salary was excellent. By the time she returned to the Bible Institute, she was beginning to feel independent financially. She had a thousand dollars in the bank and enough money to pay her extra expenses at the Institute that year. She was determined not to draw out any of the thousand dollars, which seemed a fortune to her. With it she planned to build her new home.

She was a woman now, in her late twenties and beginning to crave the security of her own four walls, but she had no conception of building costs. That she would learn in the near future, and to her dismay.

Meanwhile she continued her studies, still wondering if she would be successful in the mission field and a credit to her devoted friends the Freys, or "a prophet without honor" among her own Hopi people.

She left Los Angeles the following summer with mixed feelings of reluctance and eagerness. There could be no more dodging the issue; she would be expected to prove herself.

TEN

IN THE LITTLE MORE than a decade since she had returned from Riverside, there had been great changes. This time, instead of being met at Winslow and taken home in a lumbering, rickety wagon drawn by skinny desert horses, a missionary friend met her at Flagstaff and drove her to Moenkopi in an automobile.

As soon as the Freys had greeted her and made her comfortable in their home, the Reverend Frey—anticipating her needs, as usual—gave her great news.

He had been offered the buildings at Old Tolchaco Mission for eighty-five dollars. Would she like to salvage the building material for her dreamed-of house at New Oraibi, since he had no use for it?

Polingaysi's spirits soared. Here was her opportunity to begin work on her house, which had progressed only as far as a rock foundation. She had seen the old mission. It had been built at a ford on the Little Colorado River. The main buildings were of adobe construction, but there were wooden floors, studding, stringers, and other lumber, as well as numerous doors and windows which she would be able to use in her "big" house.

She accepted the offer, drawing eighty-five from the precious thousand dollars, and went to New Oraibi as soon as possible to make arrangements for the razing of the old buildings.

She hired two Oraibians to do the razing and hauling, giving them building materials in lieu of money for the work. But immediately she faced the problem of what to do with the material, once it arrived at the building site.

Her brother Matthew solved that problem. Not for nothing did the Hopis call him Little Badger—his name in Hopi actually meaning Building House Walking, that is, a badger building his house in whatever place he finds he needs one. He took material and built a barn in which to store the remainder of it. Homer, Matthew, and Alfred, now grown young men, were willing to help build their sister's house.

Polingaysi returned to Oraibi that time with willingness. The mission was within walking distance. She could do her work there and supervise the building at the same time.

But, alas, there seemed always to be a hidden hurdle. This time it was her health. She found she could not do the lifting and tugging that had been easy for her before she was thrown from the horse. Examination revealed that she had suffered internal maladjustments as well as a broken bone and that only surgery would correct her troubles.

Again, she went to Kansas, this time to be treated at the Newton hospital, and when she returned there was a restless period of recuperation before she could pick up the threads of her life again.

She was no longer fighting what seemed to be her destiny, yet she was not completely happy in her work at the mission. Her contacts with the white workers were satisfactory. She felt that she was valuable to them in interpreting Hopi messages and enlightening them as to Hopi thought on many subjects, but she found that often she was arguing with them rather than agreeing spontaneously that all things Hopi were wrong and that the missionaries' approach to the problem of religion was one hundred per cent right.

For the first time she was trying to analyze herself and her true views, as well as the Hopi people as a whole. It was not always a happy pursuit. More often than not she gave up in despair, wondering why she bothered and wishing she could return to the unquestioning childhood of the now distant past.

Yes, distant past. The days before the white man made his presence known with school and church seemed light years away. So much had happened, so fast. There had never been time to adjust to one development before another came along. Yet the old Hopis had seemed not to change at all, but to stand still, watching the sun as a way of timing their rituals, retreating to their kivas, planting their prayer sticks, as they had done since long before the coming of the Spaniards in 1540.

As her house began to take shape, she found that all her interest was centered there. All else was humdrum, to be finished and then forgotten in the excitement of watching her own walls rise.

She was in the back yard on a summer day in 1924, resting for a moment under the cottonwood tree and watching her brothers at work, when an employee of the government day school at Hotevilla rode up.

"Are you Elizabeth Ruth Qoyawayma?" he asked.

"Yes," she said, wondering why he had come.

"I've been asked to tell you that the position of housekeeper is open at the school and they'd like to have you take it, if you will."

Polingaysi's lips parted in surprise. Surprise not only at the words but at the surge of excitement they brought her. If mission work had seemed to be a door closing, this was one opening.

But she had been trained; her friends among the Mennonites would be shocked; the Freys, whom she loved, would be hurt. For a moment she stood with downcast eyes, silently praying, but hearing her heart speaking to her, "Take it, take it."

The man waited, lounging in his saddle. Polingaysi lifted her head. Her face was solemn. "Tell them I'll take it," she said.

Presenting herself to the Freys was painful, but she hurried to Moenkopi determined to tell them before they learned the news from any other source.

They were stunned at first, but after a moment they smiled. She was their dear child. They wanted her to be happy. Perhaps this would be best for her, and in this new venture, as in others, they would do all they could to help her. Their loving understanding and tolerance left her humbly grateful that in them she had true Christian friends.

She did not expect others to be so tolerant, and they weren't. Harsh criticism was voiced. She was an ungrateful backslider. She didn't deserve friendship and assistance, some of her former friends declared. They even implied that since she did not condemn her people completely for their ritual dances and their old form of worship, she was a "devil" worshiper. Others accused her of being mercenary and interested only in the money she could earn.

They had no insight into her inner qualms as she approached her new task. Would she be accepted by the Hopi people of Hotevilla, conservative as they were, after her attempt to convert them to the Christian religion? Would they fear her influence on their children and cause trouble at the school? Would they, products of the split between the Bear Clan and the Spider Clan, hold it against her that she was from Oraibi?

She found that being housekeeper entailed many duties, but she worked cheerfully and was delighted to learn that she was being considered for a teaching post. School officials had noticed her when she did substitute teaching at Tuba City and had been impressed by her alert, intelligent, ambitious personality.

However, since she had taken no examinations for government employment, she did not take the rumors too seriously. But they were more than rumors. She was asked to teach beginners and first grade.

"Never mind," she was told when she expressed fears as to her qualifications. "Teach. Take care of the rest as you go along."

"Now I am a teacher," Polingaysi told herself, entering the classroom at Hotevilla and looking into the blur of little faces that would, she knew, soon become individual problems and joys, each with its own fascinating personality. She was frightened. She had very little confidence. But she mustered a warm smile, remembering her first days at school when she obeyed instructions as best she could, not understanding a word the teacher spoke. At least she knew the language of these children. That, she reasoned, would make it easier for them and for her as well.

She soon discovered that she was forbidden to speak Hopi to the children in the classroom.

"We want them to learn English," the supervisors reminded her tartly. "Here are the lessons. Teach them—in English."

Polingaysi brooded over this method.

"What do these white-man stories mean to a Hopi child? What is a 'choo-choo' to these little ones who have never seen a train? No! I will not begin with the outside world of which they have no knowledge. I shall begin with the familiar. The everyday things. The things of home and family."

Immediately, she began putting her theory into practice. Instead of cramming Little Red Riding Hood into the uncomprehending brains of her small students, she substituted familiar Hopi legends, songs, and stories.

They all knew the song about the little squirrel that went out gathering pinyon nuts and was frightened by a drop of pitch that fell on his forehead. It was an action song, something like "Patty-cake, patty-cake baker's man." Hopi mothers, aunts, grandmothers, and little sisters sang it to the tiny tots, manipulating the children's hands as they sang.

Polingaysi taught the children English words to the old tune, then they sang it together.

Squirrel, squirrel, picking pinyons.
Squirrel, squirrel, picking pinyons.
Down falls pitch on his forehead.
He spills his pinyons;
Scatters his pinyons!
Then he picks, picks, picks
Up his pinyons,
And parches them,
And parches them,
Then eats, eats, eats them.

The children became little squirrels. Led by the teacher they picked imaginary pinyon nuts from imaginary trees, felt the sticky pitch on their foreheads, tossed away the nuts in alarm, picked them up again, parched them, stirring them with a stick, then stuffed the imaginary tidbits into their mouths, puffing out their cheeks with realistic fervor.

They loved it and so did Polingaysi. It was her first real taste of success. The Navajo children at Tuba City had been docile and interesting, as well as intelligent and artistic, but these children were of her own people. Hopis. She understood them. They understood her. She and they were from that day in rapport.

There were other action songs. The burrowing owl song. The prairie dog song. The coyote song. She had a feeling the missionaries would frown on the burrowing owl song which began, "We are little burrowing owls, children of Germinating God . . ." But she was surprised when the Hopi parents objected to her method of teaching.

"What are you teaching our children?" they complained. "We send them to school to learn the white man's way, not Hopi. They can learn the Hopi way at home. Why should they go to school to learn about little squirrel picking pinyons? All Hopi children know about him."

She tried to explain what she was attempting to do; how simple and easy it was to draw them out by letting them take part in the teaching. It was not difficult for them to learn English equivalents of these familiar words. They were building a vocabulary based on simple things of home and mesa, things they understood.

Reach them, then teach them, she reasoned, remembering how long it had taken her to learn to say "Jesus loves me, this I know."

She played games with the children during recess and the noon hour. She gave them responsibility in the classroom, especially recognizing the withdrawn, slow-learning ones, in an attempt to make them feel their worth to her and to the other children in the room.

With the children she could be herself, and she saw plainly that she must try to help them blend the best of the Hopi tradition with the best of the white culture, retaining the essence of good, whatever its source.

She had been taught from infancy to distrust the aggressive, pushing, loud-voiced white man, but experience had proved to her that all white people were not self-seekers bent on exploiting the Hopi people. Even so, she looked at the white teachers with whom she worked and wondered, her feelings concealed behind the Indian mask, how they felt toward her. Were they sympathetic, like the wonderful, loving, understanding Freys, like Elizabeth Schmidt, like many of her teachers at Riverside, Bethel, and the Bible Institute?

It was all very confusing to her. What to think? What not to think? How much of herself to give, and what risk of loss there was in giving—such inner worries had their effect on her natural spontaneity, making her seem a standoffish and often stubborn person.

Actually, she had but one consuming desire: to achieve a good life, independent of both white people and her own Hopi people, but esteemed by both. The struggle was not "to be a white man" but to keep from rejecting everything good she had gleaned at such cost of time and energy from the white man's world. She was always uneasily aware that it would not be difficult to shuck off the thin veneer of the white man's ways and return to the familiar mores of her Hopi people.

She had been called a two-heart by the Hopis because she had become a Christian. Now a few of her former Christian friends were calling her an idol-worshiper because she hung Kachina dolls of carved cottonwood root on her wall. The very Hopis who criticized her for, as they put it, trying to be a white man, brought her sifters and woven plaques they had made for sale, exactly as they might have presented them to a white woman.

Some of the Hopis even professed to be surprised that she still liked the Hopi food of her childhood: the *piki* bread, *pikami* pudding, cornmeal mush, and the nutritious and tasty stew of mutton and hominy called *nu-qui-vi*. As though she could escape her heritage!

"Why don't you do something about that stubborn daughter of yours," the older Hopis scolded her father and mother. "It is your fault that she does not live in her own village, a wife, mother, and fire-keeper. Why don't you tell her to come home and be a true Hopi? That's all she'll ever be."

There had been a time when such comments would have caused her either to flare up in anger or to melt into tears of self-pity. Now she could dismiss them as completely unimportant, while retaining her respect for the teaching she had received from her elders in what was beginning to seem another life ago.

"A true Hopi is a part of the universe and must keep himself in balance," she had been told. "All things, animate and inanimate, have life and being. A true Hopi tries to be aware of the deep spiritual essence that is at the heart of all things. All things have inner meaning and form and power. The Hopi must reach into nature and help it to move forward in its cycles, harmoniously and beautifully."

She had been taught to be helpful and generous. She knew the Hopi idea of responsibility to oneself. One's family, clan, community, and race. To be in harmony with the true Hopi way would help all people, she had learned early in life.

"When you make your morning prayers, breathe a wish that your life will be good. Those who have something good to live by want to live a long life. Those who are happy sing. Sing as you run to your gardens at dawn. Sing as you work in the sunshine. Do not allow anger to poison you. Thoughts of anger toward another open ways into the angry one's life through which bad influences find their way."

It was a beautiful way of thinking. Had the white missionaries ever examined those Hopi sayings with tolerance? She could see, after years of study, that the effort to change from one culture to another, from one religion to another, is almost certain to be attended by strife.

For embracing a new idea, beautiful though it was, Jesus was crucified.

Miss Burkholder continued to work with her, preparing her for an examination for Indian Service teachers which she would soon be asked to take. Polingaysi was gaining confidence as the weeks passed and the Hopi storytelling month of December came along. Again she brought the familiar into the classroom. Stories would be told in the rock houses these cold nights. She could imagine the eager little faces in the firelight and hear the crunching of parched corn and pumpkin seeds as the storytellers addressed their audiences.

"Story," she wrote on her blackboard one morning, explaining the word and spelling it for her pupils. "Who wants to tell a story?"

Hands went up. A child was selected and a legend was self-consciously told, often with help from classmates.

"Who told you this story?"

"My uncle."

"Very well. We will write the word 'uncle' on the blackboard. What was the story about?"

"A frog."

"Where did the frog live?"

"He lived in a spring."

"What did he do?"

"He sang a song about the rain that was coming to water our gardens."

"Fine. We will write the word 'frog.' Now we will make a sentence. 'My uncle told me a story about a frog.'"

When the children had read the short sentence Polingaysi enlarged upon the idea.

"My uncle told me a story about a frog that sang a song about the rain that was coming to water our gardens."

Rain, water, and other moisture words were familiar to her pupils. It was not difficult to make up an entire spelling lesson from such a story. It was also easy to relate the words to a simple lesson in arithmetic.

"How many times did the frog sing the song?"

"Four times."

"How many uncles have you?"

"Three."

"How many frogs were there?"

"One."

Then the children would make marks on the blackboard to show how many times the frog sang the song, how many uncles the little boy had; and it was not work, but fun.

Before the Christmas vacation loomed, Polingaysi's pupils were saying whole sentences in English. They could spell simple words and were learning numbers. Her pride in them knew no bounds.

With the help of the Hotevilla day school principal and others, Polingaysi passed her Indian Service test. Now she was a bona fide employee of the government.

ELEVEN

No LONGER on trial, having passed the test of the examination, Polingaysi entered into a period of comparative self-confidence. But she was not confident enough to discontinue her routine of study. There would be summer school in Flagstaff after school closed on the reservation. She meant to be ready for it, able to hold her own with the white schoolteachers.

During the week, she lived in a small cottage near the school at Hotevilla; on weekends she went to Oraibi to work on her house.

Then she fell in love. Not with a man—with a piano. It had been one of her greatest joys to visit at the home of one of the few white women in Oraibi, a Miss Olson, and play that fortunate woman's Schumann piano.

Polingaysi's father had helped freight the piano in its big wooden crate from Winslow, on the railroad, over the rough desert roads and across the dangerous quicksands of the Little Colorado River. It was only by the rarest of good luck, he had told his daughter, that the instrument reached Oraibi undamaged.

As far as Polingaysi was concerned, that piano was one of the most precious things in Hopiland. Its mellow tones struck harmony in her worried young mind. Listening to it, or playing it herself, she could forget her conflict. Her roots were deep in the homeland of the Hopi. She felt a constant pull, an attraction that held her like a magnet here on the mesas. But her own people were critical and scornful, seemingly determined not to understand her or her motives. Would they ever again include her in their closely knit community, or would she live among them an outsider, like the white man? She had crossed the bridge from her Indian world to the world of the white man; could she come back?

Under the spell of music she lost many of her fears, if only temporarily, and was in harmony with the universe. When Miss Olson was suddenly transferred to California, Polingaysi was desolate. There were no other pianos in the village. She could not afford one. Unless—unless Miss Olson would sell hers, rather than ship it. She was reluctant to ask, having very little money and being pushed to the limit to build her house, but when Miss Olson offered the piano to her at an absurdly low price for such a fine instrument, she took a deep breath for courage and bought it.

But where on earth could she store it? Her house had walls, but no roof. There was no room for such a large piece of furniture in the tiny home of her parents. Until the day set for its removal from Miss Olson's house, she worried about storage of it. Then one of the teachers at the Oraibi school offered to give it house room for the use of it. Gratefully, Polingaysi placed the piano in her care and urged the boys to roof the house with all speed.

Everyone had been working on her house—the boys, her father, sister Anna. Still it went up slowly, partly because Polingaysi was not content with a small "Hopi" house. She wanted room, lots of room, in her home.

The village gossips had a field day with her latest venture, the piano purchase.

"Where will your proud daughter put a piano?" they asked her mother. "Will she carry it around with her?"

"Maybe she will make you carry it on your back, as you would carry her babies if she had any," another wit said slyly.

The story got around and the villagers laughed. One wag, with nothing more constructive to do, drew a picture on a rock near the village. It showed an old Hopi woman bent beneath the weight of a piano. Sevenka was humiliated. Polingaysi was furious. She knew only too well that the villagers, unable to influence her directly, were taking out their spite on her by persecuting her defenseless parents.

The attitude of the villagers made her the more determined to provide well for her parents. Here she was, well dressed and with money enough to buy a piano—an instrument she had only dreamed of owning—and her aging mother was still wearing the traditional blanket dress of the Hopi woman.

"When I get my own house built," she vowed secretly, "I'll build them a new rock house. A warm and well-built one, with some of the modern conveniences."

Polingaysi sometimes realized that she was forever on the defensive, both with her own people and the white people. Sometimes she looked at her former classmates, long since married and with growing families. Living in what she now considered squalor, they were placid and happy, grinding corn in the old way, weaving their plaques, and fashioning their yucca sifters and baskets.

She tried to put herself in the place of one of these Hopi matrons. What would it be like to greet the sunrise untroubled? Surely it would be bliss. But that particular sort of bliss would never be hers, she was certain. She had too many objectives to reach, though each one meant another long and heartbreaking struggle.

"Let my people laugh," she thought defiantly, her black eyes alight with determination, a picture of the derisive Hopis in her mind. "I'll show them. I'll reach my goals in spite of them."

They laughed, looking at the size of the house she was building—she, an unmarried woman. They laughed harder when she added a bathroom to her floor plan and had pipes laid for water.

"Where's she going to get water for that big house of hers?" they asked each other. "There's no water in the other houses of the village, and no one knows when it will be brought to the village."

Polingaysi's reaction was to build a kitchen sink and install lavatories in each bedroom. Many years later water was brought to the village. Polingaysi was one of the first to apply for a permit to use it. "You white people taught us sanitation," she told the government authorities, "now make it possible for us to practice it. My house is ready for water. Please connect it with the supply."

But Polingaysi was not happy with her house. She moved her piano into the living room and took up housekeeping with pride, but the look of the house bothered her. Its hip roof of galvanized iron was not in harmony with the village of flat-roofed rock houses. They blended into the landscape like extensions of the rosy earth itself. Her house stood out, raw and unlovely.

Besides, it was not large enough. Within a year or so she had the roof torn off, added more rooms, and found new joy in it when it began to look like a pueblo dwelling.

"The first design was a resisting of the Hopi culture," she told herself in a moment of enlightenment. "It didn't belong here. This one does. But it is still not large enough. I shall add more rooms . . . someday."

Always there was that something else beckoning. Her work could not be finished and let go. There was always an overlapping of interests—a new thing coming in before the old was finished.

TWELVE

The woman on the mesa shaded her eyes, looking down onto the slope that fanned out from the sandstone cap. From this rooftop, this still-solid portion of the ruins of her grandmother's house, Polingaysi could see her big house in the new village. After several additions, it was still growing. It was in harmony with the desert now, painted in soft earth colors, with chimney pots on the roof.

It was more than a house. It was a visible part of the child with the matted hair who had stood in the fire pit that rainy night. It was part of the frightened schoolgirl; it was a part of the scolded, ridiculed, rejected young woman. It was a part of everything she had ever been or would be.

Slowly, still immersed in her thoughts, she descended the stone steps and taking a rambling route wandered close to the kiva of the Snake Clan. Suddenly realizing where she was, she felt the reaction of old superstitions raising goose pimples on her arms.

In fancy she heard again the clear call of the village crier drifting across the mesa:

"Ye dweller of the north arise; ye dweller of the west arise; ye dweller of the south arise; ye dweller of the east arise."

She could imagine how the people had looked, back in her early childhood, as they obediently came out of their houses to stand on terraced roofs and listen to words that would bring stabs of fear to each heart. "In sixteen days people of Snake Clan will give their courageous, beautiful hearts. From now on, let no one hold anger against any person. With happiness and hope, let us go forward."

Vividly, as she paused near the meeting place of the ones who had been consecrated to the presentation of the annual Snake Dance, she remembered a day when she, a small girl, had gone to the garden with her brothers. She was playing peacefully while the boys hunted rabbits with their bows and arrows. Suddenly one of the boys cried out, "Run! Run!"

She looked up, and turned cold with fright. Snake priests, searching for reptiles to carry back to their kiva, were nearby.

She looked for her brothers. They were running like little antelope toward the shelter of the rocks. Should a snake priest catch one of them and wrap a live snake about his neck, claiming him for Snake Fraternity, there would be no appeal. The boy would be initiated into the fraternity forthwith.

Polingaysi was slightly less nimble than her fleet-footed little brothers, and besides she had wanted to retrieve her little *wigoro,* cached in the shade of rabbit brush. She snatched it up and ran, clutching it to her, but stubbed her toe and went sprawling, breaking the precious *wigoro* and spilling the water into the thirsty sand.

Jumping up, heart thumping painfully, she instinctively caught the skirt of her blanket dress together, holding it tightly about her trembling legs. Should the snake gatherers approach her, she would pull her dress up, exposing her legs. They would not dare to touch her, she knew, for men of the Snake Clan were pledged to avoid women during the period of the dance and for four days afterward.

She had been safe. The gatherers were running away from her, instead of toward her. Her brothers had come out of their hiding places to continue their hunting, but she had gone home weeping over her *wigoro*.

Her older brother, the one who was too ill to attend school, had been promised to a Snake chief as a last resort to restore him to health. Had he regained his health, as his parents had hoped, he would have become a member of Snake Fraternity.

"Why must our people dance the snakes?" she had asked her mother, after being comforted over the loss of the *wigoro*. "Is there not great danger?"

From the quick turn of her mother's head, she knew she had opened a subject Sevenka preferred not to discuss. However, after a moment of silence, Sevenka shifted her bulk on the plastered floor and said, "There is a danger, my daughter. But, if we keep our hearts pure, we will be protected. All of us, including the dancers. During the days of the ceremonial dance, the dancers are accepted by Snake People."

A visiting neighbor spoke up at that point.

"There is a legend about Snake Woman and her children," she began.

Sevenka, the informed Coyote Clan woman, hissed her to silence.

"Careless one! That story must not be told in summertime. Surely your mother taught you that. It is not safe to tell it until winter has come and the little brothers are safely asleep underground." Her black eyes had darted glances into the corners of the room as she spoke, as though she feared she might see beady eyes staring at her.

It was Polingaysi's uncle who had told the girl long ago the story of "planting water" and the ordeal of one of her own ancestors who had been a water priest.

"After a rainmaker, a water priest, had lived a pure life for four years," he had informed her, "he would be ready to make his long journey to some lake or pond formed by good, sweet water from a natural spring. From this reservoir he would fill his clay transplanter jar.

"But, first, he would have sat through many secret meetings in the kiva of the rainmakers, and he would begin and continue his dangerous and lonely journey with prayers and ritualistic actions, for anything connected with water is, as you know, sacred. The spirits are always watching those whose duty it is to bring new water to the springs.

"When, after his journey, he found the sweet water, he would push into his transplanter jar, with a prayer feather, bits of moss and any water bugs that he saw in the water. Then he would fill the jar and start homeward, planting a breath feather as a prayer for good to the water serpent who 'owned' that spring or pond, and from whom he had 'borrowed' the water.

"Once the rain priest started homeward," her uncle told her, "he could not stop to rest along the way. Often Hopis run great distances, and a rain priest had to be a good runner for he had long distances to travel. He dared not set his transplanter jar of water down on the ground until he reached the failing spring in which it was to be 'planted.' To set it on the ground would be to allow the essence of the water to be transferred to that spot, and his entire trip would be fruitless.

"Immediately upon reaching the failing spring, he would place the transplanter jar in it, with proper prayers for the spring's renewal. Once it was placed, it must not be touched or removed. Very bad things would happen to anyone who touched it.

"Then, too, the rain priest must be a strong man and a good one, for he must not go near his wife or any other woman for four weeks after his return home. To break this rule would be to bring a terrible death upon himself and the woman. It is said," he told her in a confidential tone, "that the guilty ones would bloat up like bladders and act like snakes, squirming and twisting, and even hissing. Also, if he had not performed all the rituals with exactness, he or someone of his family would be charmed by water snake.

"Now," the old man had gone on, encouraged by Polingaysi's rapt attention, "I shall tell you the story of the rain priest's ordeal many, many moons ago.

"It was summer. The rain priest was on his prayerful journey to a spring on the slopes of the Snowy Heights. He was trotting along, carrying his netted jar, when a raiding party of enemies surprised him. They were on horseback.

"His captors forced this poor rain priest to run beside their horses all day without rest. His tough, leathery feet became blistered by the hot sand and rocks. He was dried up for lack of water, exhausted by hunger, fast lapsing into a state of numbness. He knew he could not live much longer. He begged for mercy, but his enemies taunted him.

" 'Coward of a Hopi!' " they said. " 'You and your people boast about being able to bring rain. Do that thing now, or be killed. We must have water, and it seems all the springs in your miserable country have dried up.'

"The rain priest was glad to have the opportunity to save himself. When they allowed him to stop he fell to his knees and began praying earnestly. He prayed to Great Being. He prayed to Good Spirit. He cried out his anguish and fear to Rain People, Cloud People, and all the unseen forces of moisture, to come to his aid.

"At last he remembered that he had concealed a breath feather in the pouch of sacred cornmeal that hung from a buckskin thong about his neck. He breathed his prayer on it and, looking up at the sky-piercing peaks of Nu-va-da-ka-o-vi, he appealed to the Kachina People.

" 'Save me now,' he prayed. " 'I offer you this prayer, my life, my self.' He released the feather. It drifted away on a breeze that lifted it and carried it toward the peaks.

"For a moment he watched it, hope in his heart, then he began to dance, and to chant deep in his dry throat the old wordless chants of the Hopi. So thin, so old, so weary that he was scarcely more than a shadow in the sunlight, he danced. He danced until a swoon like death came over him. He did not know when he crumpled and fell to the desert floor, face upward.

"When he awakened, it was to feel water striking his face. He was lying in a puddle and rain was coming down in great cool gusts. Thunder was crashing and lightning was darting its snake tongues across the black clouds.

" 'Thank you, Rain People,' " the old man quavered, sitting up. " 'Thank you. Thank you. How beautiful is the moisture. You have saved me. Now my enemies must let me go free.' But, when he looked about for them, there were none to be seen. They had been frightened away by the miracle.

"Soon the rain slackened and stopped. Clouds drifted away, all but one, a little feathery one that hovered over the peaks as the old rain priest walked homeward in the evening light."

Much superstition was mixed in the culture pattern of the true Hopi, yet there was good in it also. Walking in the silence, on the pale sand of the mesa top, the fitful wind caressing her, then rudely pushing her, by turns, Polingaysi admitted to herself with some sadness that this was a dying culture. The pattern had long ago been broken. What would be left of it after another fifty years?

The kivas of other villages would fall into disuse, as had those of Old Oraibi. No longer would smoke spiral upward from old chimney pots that sat beside the reaching arms of pole ladders. No longer would dancers stamp and chant in the plazas. As other sacred shrines vanished from their central locations, the spirit would leave the villages.

How could she, insignificant as she was in the scheme of things, bring her people a realization of the good in their old culture, now that she had finally realized it herself? Could she, perhaps, help to blend the best of the Hopi culture with the best of the white culture, retaining the essence of good from both?

There were the little children. With them the work of blending should begin. She had done what she could in the classroom, during her long career as a teacher.

THIRTEEN

THERE WAS A DAY when six men drove up to the Hotevilla school. One of them was Henry Roe Cloud, a Winnebago Indian. He was an educator with the Indian Service, and with the others was doing a field survey of schools on the Hopi reservation.

Polingaysi trembled with apprehension, but she was soon calmed by his genial, understanding, friendly approach. He, himself, would study her classroom procedures, he told her, and within a few minutes she felt at ease with him. She was able to go ahead with her teaching in her usual casual manner. She was playing a game with the children, the game of learning.

Her children had built a miniature mesa-top pueblo in the sandbox and were peopling it with small clay figures. The figures were supposedly busy at various familiar tasks. One carried wood for the *pikami* pit fire. Another drove a burro. Another meditated on a rooftop. Each was familiar to the children of Hotevilla. She could not go amiss by teaching from the familiar to the unknown. There was relation, for instance, between burro, horse, automobile, train, airplane. Also between fire sticks, trees, lumber, wooden houses.

Roe Cloud was immediately interested. He was impressed with the easy way she had of leading the children from Hopi to English. The little ones were too absorbed in the game to realize they were incidentally working at learning.

"Of all the classrooms I have visited," he told her later, "yours is the most outstanding. Your children are the most cooperative and happy. Under your instruction they are learning both eagerly and rapidly."

That was in late March of 1927, when she had been teaching for three years. She never forgot the man nor his kind words. To her they shone like bright stars in the dark sky of her terrible uncertainty. He reinforced her confidence with a letter which said in part:

"After meeting you and seeing the wonderful work you are doing I could not help but send you this word of appreciation. I have visited a great many Indian schools, non-reservation schools, reservation boarding schools and day schools among Indians, but I want to say that no school room has so pleased me as your own. The children were a pure delight because of their spontaneity, initiative, resourcefulness, in fact, in everything that goes to make up the normal development of the little child.

"You, as an Indian, among your own people, have a tremendously big influence over them. Coupled with this fact, you have not only the ability but the fine technical training to lead them into the joys of education and training for the coming civilized life of the Indian. I merely write this letter because I admire you very much for your work and want to encourage you in your personal life and endeavors for the uplift of your people.

"I am keenly conscious of the struggles each one of us has sometimes in loneliness to keep up the high standards which we have learned from the very best of American whites in the fine schools which we have been privileged to attend. I hope that you will never get discouraged and feel that the work is not worth while. It is infinitely worth while."

The fact that Henry Roe Cloud was also an Indian was of great importance to Polingaysi. He knew. He too had struggled. Perhaps not in exactly the same way, but probably painfully.

She was happy in her work. She loved her pupils and wanted to continue teaching among her own Hopi people, but this was not to be. After one more term at Hotevilla she was transferred to Chinle, a small community in the northeastern corner of the huge Navajo reservation near Canyon de Chelly.

Now she had a language barrier to contend with, for she did not speak Navajo and these little beginners did not speak English. But, applying all her skill and feeling a great sympathy for the children who were as helpless as she had been when she first attended school, she began to make progress. Also, she found the Navajo children as bright-eyed and intelligent as the Hopi children, and to her delight they responded with heart-warming quickness to her methods.

She taught there a year, then was transferred again, this time to Toadlena, New Mexico, not far from Fort Defiance, Arizona, and also on the Navajo reservation. Again her pupils were Navajos.

By this time Polingaysi was a woman nearing forty, and a perfectly normal woman who wanted a home, husband, and children. From her schooldays at Riverside she had shied away from men, even though in her inner heart she greatly desired their companionship and affection. She was lively and a good dancer and many men had tried to arrange dates with her, but she had been too uncertain of herself and too wary of their motives to encourage them.

Grimly she reminded herself that she was an Indian and a Hopi, and should marry a Hopi if she ever decided to marry anyone. But among her Hopi acquaintances there was no one to whom she was attracted, and the Hopi young men, influenced by their tradition-bound parents, had heartily disapproved of the Hopi teacher as a wife.

"Polingaysi! She's too high up," one of them exclaimed when it was suggested he pay court to the progressive daughter of the

Qoyawaymas. "She doesn't want to be a Hopi; she wants to be a white man."

Polingaysi flared up when a gossip repeated the remark to her.

"At least I'm not slaving my life away as other Hopi women do," she said. "Grinding corn until my back breaks, carrying water, scorching my hand on the *piki* stone, having a baby every two years—that life is not for me."

Always in the back of her mind was the knowledge that her parents would never approve of a mixed marriage for one of their children.

"Mixing the blood is not good," they had often told her seriously. "When you marry someone it should be a Hopi, and you should be married in the old Hopi way of washing the hair together."

Her home training had been strong. At Riverside, at Bethel Academy, at the Bible Institute, and during her years at Tuba City and Hotevilla, she had met many interesting men who had professed an interest in her. Most of them had been white men. She held them away, laughing off their attempts to be romantic.

But at Toadlena she began thinking seriously of marriage. She had met two young men, very different, but both appealing to her. One of them was a tall, handsome fellow, part Sioux and part French, very Indian in appearance. The other was part Cherokee but looked like a white man. When the second began suing for her attention, her interest in the first waned. For the first time in her life she allowed her femininity full sway and stopped being on the defensive.

When a proposal of marriage confronted her and a decision had to be made, Polingaysi was haunted by the thought of her parents' disapproval. She longed to be loved and wanted, her suspicions erased for all time, but, if she married this man, would he be welcomed in Oraibi? Also, could she continue to teach and still be a good wife?

It was a challenge. She faced it as she had faced other challenges, but this time it was her heart speaking. She accepted the proposal, buried the insistent thought that perhaps the time was not yet right for the blending of blood, stopped worrying because she could not think of Lloyd White as Indian like herself.

They were married in the spring of 1931 at Bloomfield Trading Post on the outskirts of Toadlena, Mr. and Mrs. Bloomfield had opened their home to the young couple. Except for thoughts of the whispering that would take place in Oraibi when news of her marriage reached the Hopi village, Polingaysi was happy and contented. Her husband did not object to her teaching. He was kind and understanding. But she began to yearn toward her own home in Oraibi. How pleasant it would be to live there in that cool and roomy place, with the cottonwood shading the big back yard! When school closed, she and her husband went to Oraibi.

Her father and mother greeted their new son-in-law warmly. They tried to make him welcome. It did not worry Polingaysi at first that others of her village remained aloof, their eyes scornfully watchful. She and Lloyd would stay through the summer, then return to Toadlena.

In Toadlena, Polingaysi had gained confidence in herself and in her teaching ability, this last brought about partly through the friendship of two women supervisors who visited her classroom frequently.

"Keep copies of your work," one of them constantly urged. "Send a copy to me. Please."

Polingaysi had no idea that they were working behind the scenes with other members of the official Indian Service staff. It was not until much later that she fully realized the flowering of this friendship.

During the years of teaching on the Navajo reservation Polingaysi had not been unmindful of the needs of her parents. She had saved money not only for her own house, but for the building of a neat rock house, complete with running water, linoleum, good beds, and other furniture, for the aging pair. By that time, their children married or away working, the Qoyawaymas were alone.

Polingaysi's enlarged house, with its upstairs bedrooms, demanded that it be used to advantage, and during summer vacations she received paying guests. No other place existed within many hot desert miles where travelers could obtain food and lodging, and before long her home was well known to those who wished to visit Hopiland in comfort.

Among her guests were Judge and Mrs. Leslie Denman and Mr. and Mrs. Charles de Young Elkus of San Francisco, who were interested deeply in Indian welfare, art, and handicrafts. The late Mrs. Harold Ickes was also a visitor at Polingaysi's home, and it was she who told the Hopi teacher that she should be teaching among her own people.

"I know it, and I want to come home," Polingaysi said, tears welling up and spilling over onto her cheeks, "but I haven't been able to get a transfer."

"We'll see about that," said the Cabinet member's wife.

What part the gracious lady played in the final outcome Polingaysi never knew, but it was not long before she received notice that she was to be transferred—not, however, to Oraibi, but to Polacca. At least she would be among her own people, and she could be at home every weekend. According to the notice, she would be transferred to Oraibi as soon as there was a vacancy.

Her marriage was not going well. She knew it could not survive. She would not fight its termination. Yet, brief and bittersweet though it had been, she did not regret it. In stepping from an ancient culture into the modern world, she had found many problems. She had been able to hurdle those of the intellect; those of the emotions were more difficult.

148

She could believe her parents' warning that she would not be able to adjust in marriage to a man whose interests were so foreign to her own. She could also realize that she had been independent too long, and had fought too hard for her precious independence, to take second place in her home. Her own people were not surprised when she and Lloyd parted.

"You should have married a Hopi," they said. "Long ago, when you were a young girl, you should have married in the Hopi way."

"You see!" Hopi parents told their young people. "Intermarriage doesn't work out. If anyone could make a success of such a marriage it should have been Polingaysi, who has lived so long among white people and knows their ways."

Polingaysi's parents, as usual, were kind and quiet. They uttered no barbed comments. They had warned her, but she had gone her headstrong, stubborn way, as always. If she suffered as a result, they were sorry; there was nothing they could do about it. As she had often told them, no one else could live her life for her.

The day school and community buildings of Polacca were near the old Polacca spring. About eight hundred feet above it, on a narrow tongue of rock called First Mesa, were the picturesque villages of Walpi, Sichomovi, and Hano. Like Old Oraibi, about twenty miles westward, the village houses seemed to be a part of the mesa's rocky cap. Strangers were often unaware of the villages until they caught a glint of light on a windowpane, or saw smoke rising from the chimneys. Then, looking up from the valley road, they made out the uneven outlines of the terraced rock houses.

Polingaysi's first project in the new location was to win the confidence of the Polacca people. Because she did not speak the Navajo language, she had been unable to make the acquaintance of the parents of her Navajo pupils. There was no such barrier here. She began visiting the homes on the mesa and whenever possible learned the problems of her students. In this she was successful. Because of her interest, the parents liked her. The result was increased confidence from the children.

An established and recognized teacher now, after more than a decade in the classroom, Polingaysi no longer shivered in her shoes at the approach of white educators, nor was she any longer afraid of the condemnation of her own Hopi people.

From her first days as a teacher, Polingaysi had been convinced that since the vital interest of Hopi children coincided closely with their spiritual nature and their seasonal activities, their lesson topics should be organized into sequential patterns and experiences suited to their development.

Harvesting and storing of foods would engage their interest when school opened in the fall. The winter Kachina dances and the retelling of ancient legends would be natural topics during the cold months. Gathering of wild greens, foot racing, games, and planting of familiar seeds would provide lessons for spring and early summer. Food familiar to the Hopi would provide year-round topics.

She had encountered what seemed to her a surprising amount of opposition, somewhat offset by the enthusiastic approval of such educators as her Toadlena supervisors. At one stage of her career, when she had been called to account because of her insistence on teaching from the known to the unknown, a Washington official, impressed by her logic, had defended her.

"There should be no parrot learning," Polingaysi had declared then, remembering her own parroting school days and their fruitlessness and confusion.

During her early days at Hotevilla the Hopi parents themselves had caused trouble for her by objecting to her methods, saying they did not want her to teach their children about things they already knew. A Bakabi chief had consoled her. Hobbling over to her after the meeting, he had taken her hand gently in his dry and withered palm, saying, "Daughter, do not allow them to down you. You are right."

It was Indian Commissioner John Collier who eventually gave her the greatest support. Overnight, and to the consternation of teachers confirmed in the old way of teaching Indian children, he changed the procedure.

Instead of thinking of them as "benighted children of nature," who must be "redeemed from the darkness of their superstitions and ignorance," he thought of them as worthy parts of the whole "web of life" and recognized the fact that degrading individuals may result in degrading the society to which they belong.

Instead of thinking of Indian children as people whose natural state was one of "moral and mental stupor," he recognized the dynamic inner relationship of their own culture patterns and suggested that teaching should come from within instead of without. Superimposed education, he realized, would never reach deeply into the Indian consciousness.

FOURTEEN

WHEN, after two successful terms at Polacca, she was transferred to Oraibi, Polingaysi returned with renewed confidence to her own village, only to find that she faced the fate of most prophets.

The resistance was partly brought about because another teacher, much liked by the Oraibi teaching staff, had been transferred to make room for her.

"Who is this Mrs. White?" some of the teachers asked angrily. "Why is she so important?" They were prepared to dislike her.

Not so the principal, Guy Dickerson. He received her with warm friendliness.

Unkind things were said about her. Her marital unhappiness was raked up and callously discussed, and stories were relayed to her by well-meaning friends. Though she should have been happy, since she had gained her objectives as to method of teaching and choice of village, she became more and more despondent. The fact that both Guy Dickerson and his wife were part Indian made no impression on her at the time. They were not as dark as she was.

She became silent, introspective, brooding. Once more she was trapped in a spider-web structure of suspicion, based on her own fears. The more she tried to push it away, the more entangled she became. The sense of rejection which had haunted her all her life bowed her spirit down with grief. Because of her Hopi heritage, she told herself, she would never be fully accepted by the white world, and her own Hopi people resented her interest in that world and her ability to work in it. Which way could she turn?

The many joyous experiences of her lifetime, the many times she had won through to her goals with honors in the face of opposition, the very solid achievements she had to her credit in the field of education, the backing of white friends and the approval of the Indian parents of her pupils mattered not at all in her depression. Nothing cheered her. Feeling that she was a failure, she began to dread each new day.

Finally, in desperation, she reverted to the Indian way. On a spring evening after a particularly trying day when sharp words had been spoken by some of the other teachers and what she considered to be unjust accusations had been made, Polingaysi left her big house and walked rapidly to the south, and into the desolate stretch of shifting sand dunes.

At one time, according to legend and anthropological findings, ancestors of the present Pueblo people had lived in the Oraibi valley, along what had probably been a gentle and meandering stream. Now the waterway was deeply incised and blowing sand piled up in dunes. The wind was continually pushing the sand aside to reveal artifacts. Potsherds were scattered in abundance all over the area. Polingaysi herself had uncovered whole pots there, pots that must have been in use many centuries before.

Few people visit the dunes. The teacher, bursting with resentment, disillusionment, heartache, and despair, was alone. A small figure against the towering walls of wind-rippled sand.

She stopped beside the old tree that struggled, year in and year out, against the cutting grains of sand and tearing winds that seemed determined to remove it from its station. Standing there, her hand on the rough bark of the cottonwood, she questioned herself.

Who was she? Why did she keep on struggling, struggling?

Why should other people be so cruel? Why should they be jealous of her who had never wanted to make anyone jealous? She had so little. No money except her small salary. Her hard-won house. Her inadequate education. Why should she keep on trying so hard to accomplish something in her lifetime? She was tired to death itself of fighting.

Suddenly, emotions overwhelming her, she flung herself face downward on the sand, clutching in anguish at Mother Earth, as though she must, must, have something good and sound and familiar to cling to. Not for anything in the world would she have allowed anyone to see her like this, helpless and despairing, but alone in the dunes she could open the floodgates of her emotions and thereby cleanse her spirit.

Gradually the storm spent itself. Tearstained, Polingaysi sat up, opening her hands to allow the clutched sand to run out. Some of the grains clung to her moist palms and she made a movement to brush them off, but was arrested by the colors of the grains. Sniffling a little, blinking back the last of her tears, she looked more closely. Those particles! How beautiful they were. How varied their colors. Red, tan, yellow, pink, white, black, gray, brown. Each different in size, color, and construction perhaps, but combining in all their variety to make up the great pinkish masses of the dunes.

Sand, earth, her thoughts ran on, necessary to the world as people are necessary. As she was necessary? Wasn't she a part of the "pink dune" of humanity, and therefore of worth in the over-all scheme of things?

Thoughtfully she brushed the sand from her hands, dried her eyes, blew her nose and tidied the loosened strands of her hair, then got resolutely to her feet.

"All right," she promised herself. "I won't run away from anyone any more. They don't know what they're doing to me. They're not really mean people. They don't intend to hurt me. I mustn't get so angry with them. Instead I must find a way to help them to understand me. But how?"

Through her mind flitted the Hopi tenet of nonresistance. Don't fight. Don't think spiteful things about others. Don't try to get even when they hurt you. To seek revenge is to hurt yourself more than you hurt them.

She thought that over as she walked slowly homeward. That was in essence the teaching of the missionaries. Turn the other cheek. Love those who despitefully use you. Yet, strangely enough, the missionaries had been unable to see any good in the Hopi culture pattern whose teachings were so similar.

"I'm sorry they cannot see those truths," Polingaysi thought, "but I am grateful to them. Because of them I do not await the coming of Our Brother as my unconverted people do. For me, and many others, He has come. I have given Him my heart and soul; what have I to fear, except my own lack of understanding?"

The sun was setting. Long shadows slid across the wash and up the gilded mesa to the east. The desert air was still and sweet. Through the stillness came a voice. It was the call of the village crier, making an announcement. That thread of sound reached out to Polingaysi, calling to her, binding her to her people with its familiar accents, bringing her to a realization of her duty to her students, and to her employers.

That was truly the turning of the tide. As so often happens, she had but to lay down her arms, stop suspecting everyone of malice in the making, and the entire situation smoothed out.

The next day a supervisor came to her classroom. "What have you planned for today?" she was asked.

"In keeping with my 'Happy Home' chart, I'm taking the children on a field trip. We're going to search for signs of spring. Would you like to come with us?"

"I'd love to," said the supervisor.

The little ones were delighted at the prospect of a trip. Scattered out on the sandy slope, the teacher and supervisor in the center, they walked toward Oraibi Wash below the school.

"What are we looking for?" the teacher called.

"We are looking for signs of spring," the children chorused.

"Who has found a sign of spring?"

"I have. It is a blade of green grass."

"I have. I have found ants making a new anthill."

"What color are the ants?"

"The ants are red."

"As you can see," Polingaysi told the supervisor, "we are developing a vocabulary. This is within the scope of their everyday experience, yet presented this way it becomes an adventure and they are discoverers. You will see how we correlate this excursion with the learning of English, writing, spelling, drawing, and mathematics, as well as with reading."

Just then she saw the newly made opening of the home of a ground spider. All Hopi children, reared in typical Hopi homes, know legends of wise old Spider Grandmother. Becoming all Indian herself in her desire to reach the interest of the little ones she was guiding, Polingaysi went down on her knees, calling, "Oh, come. Come. Here is Spider Grandmother's home. This is a spring sign, too."

The children came running to crowd about her as she bent over the smooth, round hole in the ground, calling in coaxing accents, "Spider Grandmother! Oh, you magic Spider Grandmother, please give me your corn mush."

The little ones laughed in delight and some of them followed their teacher's example before they wandered on down the slope.

"This is the way we learn about Nature, while learning words," Polingaysi confided. "There's something down here I want to show them. I do hope the sun hasn't destroyed it."

The something was at the bottom of the wash. A tiny stream flowed there, through thickets of willows, tenderly greening. An occasional leafless cottonwood towered. High, sandy, overhanging walls cast deep shadows where remnants of winter lingered.

"Look, children," the teacher directed them. "See those designs on the sand beside the stream. Are they like the designs you see on your windowpanes on cold mornings? This means that cold has been in the wash during the night. The *Bahana*—the white man—calls the little frost boy Jack Frost. What shall we call him?"

"Jack Frost Boy," they chorused, squatting to see more closely the beautiful traceries of the frost, and to ask, "Where are you, Jack Frost Boy? Come draw some more pictures for us."

"He must be an artist," Polingaysi said. "Don't you think so?"

They returned to the schoolroom, brimming with ideas. She gave them a few minutes of rest, then said, "Now tell me, on paper, what you have seen."

On the upper halves of large sheets of newsprint the children drew pictures of their trip. Some drew pictures of the walls of the wash and the fernlike traceries of the frost. Others drew anthills with ants running about, or spider pictures, or other scenes they had observed and enjoyed. Each expressed what was in his mind without help or hindrance from Polingaysi, then brought the result to her for help in writing below the picture the story it expressed.

Afterward, the pictures with their printed stories were tacked up and admired. Each child, with the teacher's help, read the story he had written.

"In the fall," Polingaysi told the supervisor, "we use harvest ideas. One day we may have a watermelon party. We sketch the melon, then divide it and eat it. We write descriptive words about it—smooth, round, green, cool, sweet, perhaps. We count the seeds in each portion of melon. We list the uses for the seeds. They can be parched and eaten. They can be used to oil the *piki* stone, and so on.

"We talk about home life. We take the child's own home experience as a basis and use it to teach him about the larger community life, and we go on from there to teach him about the state, nation, and world. In that way he becomes aware of his relation to life and his responsibility as an individual."

How well she taught, how much her methods were appreciated by those in higher circles of education became apparent when she was chosen from all the Indian Service teachers in the nation to demonstrate her teaching methods at the 1941 summer session in Chemawa, Oregon, before a gathering of supervisors and teachers from the United States and Alaska.

She accepted this as one more challenge, but arrived in Chemawa in an actual state of fear and trembling.

"How can I do it?" she asked herself, wishing she could race back to Oraibi in anonymity. "Will these teachers understand my methods? Will they think they can make use of them?"

They did understand. She demonstrated successfully, and at the conclusion was in a state of collapse, so great had been the strain.

On the return trip to Arizona she thought back over the years of her stubborn resistance, back to her first classroom days at Hotevilla in 1924, and she laughed at herself. She had been so positive her approach to teaching had been correct. She knew it was right, because the way she had been taught was so very wrong.

She had proved herself, not only in the Chemawa demonstrations but throughout the years of her teaching, and it was clear to her finally why Henry Roe Cloud and other government officials had spent a great deal of time in her classrooms during their inspection tours. She could also understand why her beloved inspector at Toadlena had insisted that she retain copies of her "Happy Home" chart.

No doubt it had seemed strange to them at first to hear a

teacher ask her pupils to set the study course for the day and to impose their own rules of conduct on their classmates, but they had eventually seen the wisdom of it.

For one thing, it had made the children, young though they were, aware of their responsibility to themselves, their teacher, and their classmates. Once having stated their desires, it was easier for them to follow through.

The woman on the mesa stopped suddenly, her head coming up with a jerk. Hadn't she stated her desires to the Great Teacher? Wasn't it up to her to follow through?

After Chemawa, she had returned to the classroom, but with lessened enthusiasm. That experience had been the climax of her teaching years. The daily sameness of the succeeding months had been anticlimactic. She had become more and more restless. She wanted change. She needed another big challenge.

Polingaysi was surprised and thrilled when she received an invitation from Dr. T. J. Tormey, president of Arizona State Teachers College in Flagstaff, to present a program by her primary rhythm band at one of the regular college assemblies.

When she relayed the invitation to her pupils the little ones became greatly excited, though apprehensive.

"I'm afraid of white people. We might get lost in town. I don't have good shoes to wear," they worried. But fears soon gave way to anticipation.

The children carried the news home. Their mothers, immediately interested, came to the school to verify the invitations and to discuss necessary preparations.

Material for making band uniforms had been provided by the Hopi Indian Agency superintendent, but the cloth had to be made up. This was something the women of the village could do. Mothers and other relatives and friends came to help with the sewing. Members of the Girl Scouts also helped to sew the simple seams. When the first blue cape, lined with golden yellow satin, was modeled by one of the children, no doubt lingered in the students' minds about whether or not they wanted to go.

"What shall we do to get ready? We want to look just right," one of them declared, and the others agreed.

Polingaysi asked for suggestions and wrote them on the board:

> We must have clean hands.
> We must have clean faces.
> We must not have sores on our bodies.
> We must not have bugs on us.
> We must wear clean clothes.
> We must polish our shoes.
> We must have our hair cut.
> We must not be ashamed to speak English.
> We must not be afraid of white people.

They counted the weeks. They counted the days.

"Only three weeks more . . . only two weeks more." As time for the trip neared, tension mounted. "Only three days now," they told each other, eyes wide, faces shining, "until we go to Flagstaff."

Sometimes they turned worried countenances toward their teacher and asked, "Are we really going, Mrs. White?"

Polingaysi realized the responsibility of taking twenty-six little children more than a hundred miles across the reservation and into Flagstaff. The road was rough and windswept. The country was unpopulated.

She discussed the problem with the superintendent and his wife; it was decided to secure the fullest cooperation of the parents. To do this they made personal calls. They were warmly welcomed everywhere.

One mother said, "I'm glad to let my boy go. He talks about the trip every day. He wants to go."

Another said, "I never had that chance when I went to school. Yes, I want my child to go."

At the village of Old Oraibi, up on the rimrock, a Hopi father said, "It's all up to our boy. He's afraid of getting lost. My wife and I told him it would be nice for him to go."

During those visits Polingaysi and her teacher friends were impressed by the consideration of the parents for their children, and the tender warmth that existed between parent and child. It was plain to see that they loved and trusted each other.

Use of the Agency bus had been promised for transportation, and "going in the big bus" frequently cropped up in the children's conversations. Then the first disappointment came. The bus had broken down. It could not be repaired in time for the excursion. A truck would be made available instead.

The thought of taking a trip in an open truck, with all of those little children exposed to the uncertain spring weather, often very cold and blustery at 7,000-foot Flagstaff, was discouraging. Polingaysi considered canceling the visit altogether.

That evening the mothers came to Polingaysi's big house to learn the time of departure. When she told them the news they were terribly disappointed, not for themselves but for their children.

"What will the children do? They've lived for it and worked for days to get ready. They are taking baths tonight. They've washed their hair. Isn't there anything we can do?" they asked.

Polingaysi knew their little ones well. She knew how disappointed they'd be to have their hopes blasted at this last minute. It would be too much.

"We'll go!" she told the mothers. "I'll take the tiniest ones in my little car. The others must go in the truck. Be sure they're warmly dressed and have blankets to wrap up in."

On the morning of April 8, the children got up early. They arrived at the schoolhouse at six o'clock. Mothers and older sisters came with them to help them don their white dresses, and white shirts and pants, over which they proudly fastened the flashy blue and gold capes.

The children crowded in front of the big mirror in the classroom, admiring themselves; some even ran home to show their fathers and other relatives how splendid they looked. As for Polingaysi, she became the custodian of their shopping money, which they would spend in Flagstaff stores after the program.

Then the truck rumbled into the schoolyard and the children ran to climb into it. Mattresses had been placed on the truck bed and the children wrapped their warm blankets about them and huddled together for warmth, trusting the superintendent and his wife, Mrs. "Dee," to transport them safely to Flagstaff.

Polingaysi owned a small car with a cramped back seat. She crammed seven little ones into it, the smallest child, a little girl named Frances, riding astride Polingaysi's back.

At last they were off, the children singing happily. Then, desert people though they were, they got lost, taking the wrong road at the Leupp bridge over the Little Colorado and heading into the Canyon Padre country. Out there, in that desolate, rocky region of chill winds, the truck developed engine trouble. But, after a considerable delay, the little group reached U.S. Highway 66, several miles east of Flagstaff, and spirits rose again.

"Now we're on the good black road," the children exulted. As they neared Flagstaff and the desert rabbit brush and stunted juniper gave way to Ponderosa pine, one of Polingaysi's passengers cried out, "Oh, look at the trees. So big. So tall. Oh, Mrs. White!

See the tall mountains. All white on top. Is it snow? Look at the hills with nothing growing on them."

These were the cinder hills that mark the area east of Sunset Crater.

When they reached the outskirts of town the little ones began to shrink from the signs of civilization, so foreign to them.

"Houses. Lots of houses. Many cars. Many white people," they observed.

Little Frances bent to whisper in her teacher's ear, "I'm not afraid of white people."

The friendly reception given them at the college by Miss Mildred Kiefer, demonstration teacher of the primary class, helped put the chilled and weary little children at ease. After a short rest, they were seated at decorated tables loaded with goodies which immediately excited their imaginations and stimulated their appetites. Then white children came in and took places near their Hopi guests. At first only shy glances were exchanged, but before the luncheon was over Hopi and white children were happily chatting and laughing together.

Soon it was time for the program. The Hopi youngsters were awed by the size of the auditorium. Fear was written on their solemn faces.

"Maybe I get scared," one child whispered. "Look. So many seats."

When they took their places on stage and the curtain was pulled aside to reveal them in all their costumed splendor, at the same time revealing to them the upturned white faces of the audience, they blinked in something close to stupefaction. Polingaysi brought them out of their daze by playing the introduction, then their leader gave them the signal. They forgot themselves and the strange white people in playing with enthusiasm and skill their much practiced selections.

Two Hopi songs, sung first in Hopi, then in English delighted their audience and brought them soul-warming applause. Looking at them, glowing with accomplishment, Polingaysi thought of Henry Roe Cloud's letter.

"I hope you will not be discouraged and think the work is not worth while. It is infinitely worth while," he had written, and, studying the excited faces of her charges, she knew he had been right.

After the program came the anticipated and promised shopping period. The children were all but frantic at the sight of the many desirable things—all sorts of toys, Easter eggs, little yellow cotton chickens, candy, rabbits. But with such a small amount of money to spend, decisions were all but impossible. They lingered, looking and longing.

The stores in which they shopped were on the main street of the town. It paralleled the railroad tracks. When a train came whistling through, they screamed, "Train! Train!" and rushed outside to watch it pass. Some of them had never seen one.

The trip home was a quiet one. They were tired, but when they tumbled out of the truck after the long and dusty ride, they were unanimous about wanting to go again. "I made many friends. I want to go live in Flagstaff! Let's go back soon," they said, and Frances sighed blissfully, "I just do want to live in Flagstaff all the time."

FIFTEEN

POLINGAYSI'S FATHER had developed diabetes and was failing rapidly. She took him into her home, where she could give him good nursing care.

He delighted in talking to her about the old days. Amused, his eyes twinkling, he reminded her that she had followed him when she was little, but later on had taken the lead while he walked meekly behind her.

He enjoyed sitting in the shade of the cottonwood tree he had planted in what was to become her houseyard, and often he pointed out other trees, cottonwoods or poplars or fruit trees, which he had planted in the valley and on the hillside. He was proud of the lone tree in the sand dunes. It was the only remaining one of several he and his son Matthew had planted there years before. The trees, spots of green where birds might nest and weary people find shade on hot days, were growing because he had been progressive enough to see a need for them.

He had helped Polingaysi plant peaches, pears, apples, and apricots, and the trees were flourishing, though watering had cost her many a backache. She had started a vineyard, too, with his help, and the grapes were sweet. Hopi children harvested most of her fruit, but the portion she salvaged for canning was delicious.

Fred Qoyawayma was the only one of Polingaysi's family who

had not accepted the teachings of the missionaries. Finally, he too became a Christian. Being at one with his family made him very happy.

"Always I have been standing at the door," he remarked in deep contentment, "but now I can come inside with my family. No longer must I be apart from you."

He had much to remember and talk about during those days of his illness. H. R. Voth, the missionary, had recognized the Hopi man's keenness of mind and had taught him many things, among them how to deliver babies and how to serve as a dentist when Hopi teeth needed pulling.

When Qoyawayma served as dentist, he used a pair of forceps given to him by Voth. When he assisted at the birth of babies, he combined the white man's technique with the Hopi way, passing the Hopi grass brush—the *wu-u-si*—across the laboring woman's buttocks to brush away evil forces that might be delaying her delivery.

Voth had taught him to do simple carpentering, and in spite of his ignorance of arithmetic he used his small hands as measuring instruments and was remarkably accurate.

When the Indian Service sent Health Nurse Abbott to the Hopi reservation to do what she could about teaching the villagers sanitation, Fred Qoyawayma was asked to assist her, not as interpreter, for she spoke Hopi fluently, but as handyman.

Miss Abbott was a dynamo. She swept through the villages ordering the piling and burning of old goat and sheep skins, seeing to it that tin cans were gathered and dumped over the cliffs, urging the women to develop pride enough to do away with other refuse and sweep their homes and the village streets. At her urging, they also freshened their house walls with plaster. Fred Qoyawayma had to step lively to keep up with her.

For a long time after she finished her task, the results of the campaign were noticeable, especially at Bakabi, the new village which was the last to result from the Oraibi split. For several years it was cited as a model of cleanliness.

It was Voth, also, who recommended that Qoyawayma help build the Fred Harvey Hopi House on the edge of Grand Canyon. Later, when Harvey needed a responsible Hopi family as caretakers at Hopi House, Voth suggested the Qoyawaymas.

This time Sevenka objected. To live away from the Hopi villages, bereft of the daily companionship of her friends, unable to take part in Mazhrau dances and witness the Kachina ceremonies? Unthinkable!

"Besides," the sturdy Hopi woman argued, "there is no medicine man at Grand Canyon. Suppose my children get sick. Do you not remember," she asked her husband, "when they had the red sickness which claimed the life of Polingaysi's next younger sister? Do you remember how Polingaysi also nearly died, and how she lay for days in the medicine man's arms, panting like a little kangaroo mouse—a *pehu*—and more dead than alive? It was the medicine man who saved her life."

Her husband listened. He remembered. It was possible, he agreed, that they would be lonely, withdrawn from the life they had always known. They did not go.

During the last weeks of his illness Polingaysi's father often spoke abruptly, out of his silent rememberings. One day, chuckling, he said, *"Bahan-ko-wa-ko-hoya!"*

Half fondly, half derisively, the Hopi people had called him by that nickname. *Bahan-ko-wa-ko-hoya*—little white man rooster. He had no doubt jumped around very officiously at times, when carrying out the orders of Voth and other white men.

Another time Polingaysi heard him carrying on a conversation, apparently with a visitor. Wondering who it was and how anyone could have entered the house unknown to her, she went to the sick man's bedroom. He was alone.

"Just keep on crying at me like that," he was telling the unseen visitor firmly. "You're not scaring me. Go away! Don't bother me! No! No, I'm not going with you. You say I'll be crying? Well, we'll see."

"Who is it you talk to, father?" Polingaysi asked.

The dying man turned his thin face toward her.

"Masau-u," he murmured. "Didn't you hear him? He was crying at me. 'Whoo-o-o . . . whoo-o-o,' he was saying to me. He's gone now. I told him not to bother me."

Masau-u! God of Death and Destruction. Legendary owner of Oraibi! In spite of her religious knowledge, Polingaysi felt goose pimples rising on her arms.

"Lord, give me strength," she prayed, closing her eyes for a moment. But the eerie call still rang in her ears.

When her father was gone, Polingaysi realized how little she knew about him and his inner ideals and beliefs. If she could only ask him some of the things she should have asked long before. But now it was too late. She was a long time in recovering from the shock of his death, and by that time Sevenka, her hardworking, conservative Hopi mother, was ailing. In 1951 she too started on her journey to Soul's Resting Place.

The cottonwood in the houseyard was showing its age now. It had lost many limbs, wrenched off by the fierce desert gales. Its bark was thick and rough, yet it put forth its shining leaves each spring unfailingly.

Despite her black hair and unwrinkled brown skin, Polingaysi also was aging. She began to think of retiring. The thought of relinquishing the monthly salary check which had made possible the construction of her big house, and financial aid to brothers, nieces, and nephews who wished to go on to college from the local schools, was a bit frightening, but she was tired. Tired of teaching. She had been in the classroom for more than a quarter of a century. She was teaching children of her former pupils. She continued, however, until 1954. Then she gave notice.

When the Hopi mothers learned of her decision many of them tried to dissuade her.

"Please teach just one more year," they begged. "I want you to give my beginner a start."

When she finished her work in the classroom that year she expected nothing, but her retirement proved to be the occasion for a well-attended ceremony during which she was presented with a bronze medal of commendation and an honor award from the U.S. Department of the Interior.

"Elizabeth Q. White," it stated, "is hereby awarded this certificate of honor for commendable service." It was dated June 30, 1954, and was signed by Glenn L. Emmons, Commissioner, Bureau of Indian Affairs. After the exciting, emotional climax to her more than thirty-one years of teaching in the Indian Service, she was free to begin a new life.

How often she had sighed for freedom. She had a feeling for clay. When she took clay into her hands she had the impulse of the Hopi woman to shape it into articles of use and beauty. Bowls, lovely jars, round-bellied *wigoros,* or water jugs, such as the Old Ones carried on their backs. She could feel the willingness of the clay to follow the direction of her small, short-fingered hands. It challenged her to do something with it.

And there was music. For years she had felt that she should do something with her musical training—when she had the time. And surely, with all her firsthand information, she should be able to write about her people.

Now she would have the time. All the time there was. Yet she felt as though she had been plunged into a vacuum. She was lost, not knowing where to begin. Had she come to the end of her trail? She considered leaving the reservation and attempting to make a future for herself among white people, but in the depths of her being she felt the pull of the mesas and the wind-harried desert. She loved the big house she had built at New Oraibi, the village on the slope below the ruins of the pueblo village where she was born. She felt a responsibility to the many friends—writers, artists, scientists, and other Indian-conscious people—who came each summer to spend a few days or a few weeks in Hopiland. They were her contact with the world of the white man and she enjoyed them as they enjoyed her.

With the problem of what to do with her life, she had come back to the once great primitive city of Oraibi. Back to its crumbling buildings and empty streets. She had come asking herself a question, and she had found the answer.

The clay she longed to work was waiting for her in its ancient beds, tons on tons of it, ready to be transformed by her loving fingers; the old songs were still on the lips of her old people, waiting for her to capture them in notes on white paper; there was material enough about the Hopi to keep her busy for the rest of her lifetime, should she chose to write it, and there was the old house, its wings spread like a desert hen to shelter those who came seeking knowledge of her people.

Indians were not the only ones who had bridges to cross. There were white people who were trying to bridge the gap between their own culture and that of their Indian brothers. She could help them. What better way to bring about understanding between peoples than to serve as a link between them?

The old chief saw her coming back to her car, walking rapidly now. He waited for her.

"Have you found that for which you were seeking?" he asked compassionately, his gaze leaving her face for an instant to rest on the silver-framed bronze medal that hung from a silver chain about her neck.

Polingaysi smiled.

"Oh-ee," she said. "Yes."

It was true. She had found what she sought, the answer to her agonized questioning. She knew, finally, where she belonged. She had discovered that she was a free soul, not confined to one place, but free to go wherever she wished to go, as long as she went as an emissary of good will, free to accept the challenges of life, whatever they might be.

Yes, she had found her answer, and for the first time since she was a small child, she was at peace with herself.

EPILOGUE

"WE DO NOT walk alone. Great Being walks beside us. Know this and be grateful."

Many times Polingaysi had heard her mother say those words, yet during her own time of stress she had often forgotten to acknowledge spiritual assistance and the Presence. Instead, she had elected to go the lonely way, trying to accomplish through sheer determination the improvements in educational methods which she thought necessary.

At times she had felt she was the only frustrated teacher and that her years of struggle, her clashes with white educators in defense of her idea of educating Indian children from the known to the unknown, her efforts to prove that the clear light of practicality was superior to the fog of theory, had been futile. But soon after her retirement other teachers, as frustrated as she had been, began coming to her.

One man, emotionally shaken by his problem, had no more than closed the door behind him before he started to tell her his troubles. "Mrs. White, you've been through this. You should know some of the angles. What am I to do? My supervisor says I must stop teaching my pupils science and higher mathematics, because those subjects are too difficult for them and cannot be grasped by the Indian mind. But, I tell you! There's nothing wrong with the minds of my pupils. Some of them are exceptionally brilliant. They'll go far in the world if they are well trained. I've already brought them to a realization of the value of learning and they're eager to forge ahead. They're making good grades in first-year algebra. Does that look as though their brains were inferior?"

"Of course not!" Polingaysi said indignantly, looking at the teacher with new interest, now that he had exposed himself as a kindred soul. "Don't you be discouraged. Go on giving them all they'll absorb. I faced opposition for years, and I lived through it. You'll be glad you helped them. In spite of everything, it will work out well."

And it did. Several of the children who had studied under that dedicated man's instruction went on to college.

Though Polingaysi no longer stood in the classroom and had no desire to return to teaching, her work for the education of her people was by no means over. Educators came to her, asking in all sincerity for her ideas.

They discussed their problems in educating Indian children and asked what, in Polingaysi's opinion, was wrong with their methods. They told of their inability to reach the children and arouse the spark of interest.

Dared she speak up? She, who had been one of those little wild things of the mesa, with no background except that of the small rock house in the isolated village of Old Oraibi? Dared she stand up and speak her mind, bare her heart, to the authorities? Would they listen, sensing that her words were the result of long, bitter, soul-searching thought? Would they open their minds enough to accept, or at least to consider thoughtfully, what she had to say about unfortunate reactions to the white man's methods with Indian children?

Of course she would speak up. They had asked, hadn't they?

The white man killed the buffalo, she told them, because the buffalo presented a problem. Indian children are a problem too, but can't be so peremptorily disposed of. They should be regarded as valuable assets to the nation and to the world, for that is what they can be, once their talents and special abilities are recognized and encouraged.

But don't ask them to peel off their brown skins and become white men. Peel though they might, there'd always be another layer of brown underneath. No. Rather, ask them to be themselves, help them to realize the value of their own heritage. Too much time has been spent in trying to teach them to cast aside the Indian in them, which is equivalent to asking them to cease being. An Indian can no more be a white man than a white man can be an Indian. And why try? There is infinite good in the Indian culture pattern. Let's look at this thing objectively, understanding each other with charity; not disparaging the differences between us, but being gratefully aware of the good qualities we may adopt, one from the other.

The change in educational methods through the years had been tremendous, Polingaysi reflected, thinking back to her first school days: the saucer of syrup and the hardtack, the ticking dress, the stupid, brutal whippings and humiliations. She and her companions had been treated like little dumb animals because they did not speak the language of the school authorities. Now, so it seemed to her, the pendulum had swung too far to the other extreme. The Indian child was being coddled, overfed, overdressed, carried on a cradleboard, as it were, and not allowed to develop strength by standing on his own two feet.

"Always," she sighed, "the white man asks too much in the wrong way. When education is presented to the Indian child in the right manner, he will absorb it as readily as does any white child. Educate them from what they already know, not from a totally new, strange field of experience. Faced with problems completely foreign and beyond his scope, it is most certain that the average Indian child will withdraw into his shell. Not knowing how to get past the closed doors of ideas he cannot understand, yet too proud to openly lose face by admitting his lack of understanding, he may seem to his teacher quite impervious to learning.

"Lead them, guide them, but don't try to whip them into education, and don't make the mistake of thinking education can be superimposed upon them, like plaster on a wall. The quick and lasting learning comes from an understanding between teacher and child."

She had not seen these truths immediately upon entering her first classroom. She had floundered through several miserable school terms before she gained confidence in herself and her chosen, slowly worked out method of teaching and reaching her pupils. Even the Indian parents had objected to her teaching of Hopi ways as an approach to the white man's way. They had not, in their confusion, remembered that fields must be prepared for planting.

Half a century ago, Hopi people had opposed education violently; now they became aware of its many advantages. Where they had once accepted it rebelliously, they now sought it for their children.

"Tell us how we can help our children get a college education," they begged. "You gave them a good start. We want them to be able to go on, and they want to go. They want to do something with their lives, as you did."

World War II had a great deal to do with this change of attitude. Hopi young men had gone into the service poorly educated, used to the paternalism of the government, sheltered blindly from the outside world. The awakening to their place in life was in many cases a rude one, but they were intelligent, if uneducated, and they saw how much they had missed by neglecting to apply themselves in the schoolroom. They wrote letters home revealing their distress and acknowledging its cause.

"Tell my brothers to get all the education they can," they told their parents. "Tell them to be sure to finish high school and if possible to go on to college. If I had it to do over again, I'd get all the education I could. Believe me, you need education to get along in this man's world."

The plight of the young people weighed on Polingaysi's mind. Sometimes the heaviness was so great that she was reminded of her mother who, after a time of worrying, said that she felt as though she had stones in her stomach.

No one likes to be criticized, she admitted, but criticism can be something like the desert wind that, in whipping the tender corn stalks, forces them to strike their roots down deeper for security. She had been criticized by both her own people and the white people, in many cases severely. But perhaps the criticism had forced her to seek anchorage which now gave her the strength and the purpose to attempt one more advancement for her people. But it would take time.

Time. For centuries time had been of no importance to the Indian. The sun rose, the sun set. The Indian worked or hunted, danced or played, while there was light; when darkness came, he slept. No clocks had ticked in the rock homes of Polingaysi's ancient people. They lacked the white man's conception of time. There were changes of the moon, changes of the seasons; but no one counted the hours. Now the Hopi must learn to respect the busy clock and be controlled by the circuiting hands. Not to conform was to be thrown off balance. The old days were gone forever. One must face the new.

Like most Indians something of a visionary, Polingaysi dreamed of higher educational opportunities for Indian youth. No longer is the Hopi isolated. Black-topped highways thread the reservations of the West. The world finds it easy now to reach the mesas and the desert lands, and the Indians can no longer ignore the world. They are of it and must come into harmony with it, the sooner the better. There is no other way than to go forward. Education is necessary for the living of a full life in this era, and specialization requires training.

So Polingaysi mused, and from this basis began turning in her mind the thought of setting up some sort of a scholarship fund for worthy high school graduates. If Indian-conscious friends could be persuaded to contribute even small sums per year, she reasoned, and if a few boys and girls would take advantage of an opportunity to receive higher learning, the world would soon be forced to recognize the worthiness of the project.

Her own slender funds could not be stretched to cover such an ambitious project. She knew of no one who could or would finance it, but once it got going she was sure help would come. She would plant the idea; it would grow.

Two talented writers, a husband-wife team, visited Polingaysi one summer at her big home. The conversation turned to education, and before she knew it Polingaysi was enthusiastically outlining her proposed project. She talked so well that she fired the imagination of her guests. They volunteered to start the fund with a liberal donation, far beyond anything Polingaysi had hoped for.

Moved to grateful tears, she told them how delighted she was. At least one child could enter college at once, and there was a worthy girl waiting. She was the eldest of a large family and her father earned only a modest salary. She was willing to work for part of her necessities, but would need help to finance the balance. When she learned that the way had been opened for her, she was overcome as Polingaysi had been.

Thus the project was started and Polingaysi began looking around for other young people who were longing to go on but could not finance their education. She found them. One boy wanted to be a laboratory technician. He had already spent one year at pre-medical school, but now needed help. However, by the time he applied, the fund was exhausted.

"But, tell him not to give up," Polingaysi assured his worried mother. "There will be more. I know it."

While he was waiting, he went to a nearby hospital and offered his services free of charge in return for the coveted experience he would gain. He was accepted and became a valuable assistant— so valuable that the hospital heads saw to it that he received pay for his work. Then he was able to return to his studies, more convinced than ever that he had found his life work and that money would be forthcoming as he required it.

Months passed, and there was still no money in the fund, in spite of Polingaysi's faith. The first donors had pledged more, however, and it would come in due time. Meanwhile the founder went to a Hopi friend, an intelligent, energetic, and handsome woman about her own age.

"It's time we Hopi people began standing on our own feet," she said. "It's good to get help, but not if we hang back and refuse to help ourselves. Why should white people finance this movement entirely, when it is for the good of our youth? If we want something done, let's do it ourselves. It's our problem. Let's take the initiative in solving it."

Her friend wholeheartedly agreed. She was a splendid organizer. She called her friends together, outlined plans for a food and gift sale, and had them all working together immediately. The event was a social and financial success. Money was in the fund once more, but it was barely enough to meet immediate demands on it.

The word was getting around that three Hopi young people were attending college, financed by the scholarship fund. Applications for assistance began coming in. The following excerpt from one applicant's letter is an example of the quality of the applicants:

"Needless to say," the young woman wrote, "I hope to work with my people. The process of acculturation is a long one and I would like to help them along the way. I feel that as a teacher of very young people, I would be doing a job that would be very important to these little people later on in their lives. I would be a part of the constructive group that will help mold their minds to good sound thinking."

Those words struck a chord in Polingaysi's consciousness. They were almost like an echo from her own thoughts. The applicant, through secretarial work for an anthropologist, had decided her life's course. To "help the little people" to a better and less painful transition into the world of the white man—what could be more desirable? The girl must be helped.

"Aren't you expecting altogether too much of your Indian people?" one of her white friends asked Polingaysi, after hearing about her successful efforts to start the scholarship fund.

Polingaysi flared back at her.

"Absolutely not! No! I'm not expecting anything unusual from my people? It is in Hopi culture teachings that we must prepare ourselves for life. 'Get up! You must live your life from beginning to end. No one else can do it for you.' That is what the old people tell the youngsters. The fact that we now face a new way of life does not change the importance of the teaching. No one can do it for you. Coddling doesn't help, but every deserving young person should have a chance to prove himself.

"I tell the young people this: 'Your foundation is in your parents and your home, as well as in your Hopi culture pattern. Evaluate the best there is in your own culture and hang onto it, for it will always be foremost in your life; but do not fail to take also the best from other cultures to blend with what you already have. We are not a boastful people, so do not allow your educational advantages to make you feel contempt for the older ones of no education who have made your progress possible. Give them credit for the good there is in them and for the love they have in their hearts for you. Don't boast, but on the other hand, don't set limitations on yourself. If you want more and still more education, reach out for it without fear. You have in you the qualities of persistence and endurance. Use them."

The highway, which the Hopis at one time feared, will serve a double purpose. It will bring the white world closer, and gradually the Hopis and their white neighbors will learn to understand each other. With understanding will come further simplification of the problem of teaching Hopi children.

Teachers who know how the parents and grandparents of their pupils live and think will understand their pupils better and be able to work efficiently with them.

That is Polingaysi's belief. Looking back into her own confused childhood and youth, she can now feel that everything she suffered was for the purpose of leading her to the undertaking of this plan for educating the young people from the no longer isolated mesa villages.

The rapidity with which the movement blossomed, once given a start, still makes it seem a trifle unreal to her, but a great satisfaction lies in the fact that through the cooperation of college authorities and white friends the world over, and the loyal efforts of her own people, doors of higher education have been opened to Hopi young people, and will continue to open to them for years to come.

It is only fitting that Polingaysi, child of the mesas, should have been the one to start it.